MznLnx

Missing Links Exam Preps

Exam Prep for

Fundamental Managerial Accounting Concepts

Edmonds, Tsay, & Olds, 4th Edition

The MznLnx Exam Prep is your link from the texbook and lecture to your exams.
The MznLnx Exam Preps are unauthorized and comprehensive reviews of your textbooks.

All material provided by MznLnx and Rico Publications (c) 2010
Textbook publishers and textbook authors do not particpate in or contribute to these reviews.

MznLnx

Rico Publications

Exam Prep for Fundamental Managerial Accounting Concepts
4th Edition
Edmonds, Tsay, & Olds

Publisher: Raymond Houge
Assistant Editor: Michael Rouger
Text and Cover Designer: Lisa Buckner
Marketing Manager: Sara Swagger
Project Manager, Editorial Production: Jerry Emerson
Art Director: Vernon Lowerui

Product Manager: Dave Mason
Editorial Assitant: Rachel Guzmanji
Pedagogy: Debra Long
Cover Image: Jim Reed/Getty Images
Text and Cover Printer: City Printing, Inc.
Compositor: Media Mix, Inc.

(c) 2010 Rico Publications

ALL RIGHTS RESERVED. No part of this work covered by the copyright may be reproduced or used in any form or by an means--graphic, electronic, or mechanical, including photocopying, recording, taping, Web distribution, information storage, and retrieval systems, or in any other manner--without the written permission of the publisher.

Printed in the United States
ISBN:

For more information about our products, contact us at:
Dave.Mason@RicoPublications.com

For permission to use material from this text or product, submit a request online to:
Dave.Mason@RicoPublications.com

Contents

CHAPTER 1
Management Accounting and Corporate Governance — 1

CHAPTER 2
Cost Behavior, Operating Leverage, and Profitability Analysis — 14

CHAPTER 3
Analysis of Cost, Volume, and Pricing to Increase Profitability — 18

CHAPTER 4
Cost Accumulation Tracing, and Allocation — 24

CHAPTER 5
Relevant Information for Special Decisions — 29

CHAPTER 6
Cost Management in an Automated Business Environment: ABC, ABM, and TQM — 32

CHAPTER 7
Planning for Profit and Cost Control — 37

CHAPTER 8
Performance Evaluation — 43

CHAPTER 9
Responsibility Accounting — 47

CHAPTER 10
Planning for Capital Investments — 55

CHAPTER 11
Product Costing in Service and Manufacturing Entities — 61

CHAPTER 12
Job-Order, Process, and Hybrid Cost Systems — 63

CHAPTER 13
Financial Statement Analysis — 65

CHAPTER 14
Statement of Cash Flows — 78

ANSWER KEY — 84

TO THE STUDENT

COMPREHENSIVE

The *MznLnx* Exam Prep series is designed to help you pass your exams. Editors at MznLnx review your textbooks and then prepare these practice exams to help you master the textbook material. Unlike study guides, workbooks, and practice tests provided by the texbook publisher and textbook authors, *MznLnx* gives you **all** of the material in each chapter in exam form, not just samples, so you can be sure to nail your exam.

MECHANICAL

The MznLnx Exam Prep series creates exams that will help you learn the subject matter as well as test you on your understanding. Each question is designed to help you master the concept. Just working through the exams, you gain an understanding of the subject--its a simple mechanical process that produces success.

INTEGRATED STUDY GUIDE AND REVIEW

MznLnx is not just a set of exams designed to test you, its also a comprehensive review of the subject content. Each exam question is also a review of the concept, making sure that you will get the answer correct without having to go to other sources of material. You learn as you go! Its the easiest way to pass an exam.

HUMOR

Studying can be tedious and dry. MznLnx's instructional design includes moderate humor within the exam questions on occassion, to break the tedium and revitalize the brain

Chapter 1. Management Accounting and Corporate Governance

1. The _____ is a private, not-for-profit organization whose primary purpose is to develop generally accepted accounting principles (GAAP) within the United States in the public's interest. The Securities and Exchange Commission (SEC) designated the _____ as the organization responsible for setting accounting standards for public companies in the U.S. It was created in 1973, replacing the Accounting Principles Board and the Committee on Accounting Procedure of the American Institute of Certified Public Accountants. The _____'s mission is 'to establish and improve standards of financial accounting and reporting for the guidance and education of the public, including issuers, auditors, and users of financial information.'

The _____ is not a governmental body.

   a. Public company
   b. Fannie Mae
   c. Governmental Accounting Standards Board
   d. Financial Accounting Standards Board

2. _____ is the term used to refer to the standard framework of guidelines for financial accounting used in any given jurisdiction. _____ includes the standards, conventions, and rules accountants follow in recording and summarizing transactions, and in the preparation of financial statements.

Financial accounting information must be assembled and reported objectively.

   a. Current asset
   b. General ledger
   c. Long-term liabilities
   d. Generally accepted accounting principles

3. _____ is concerned with the provisions and use of accounting information to managers within organizations, to provide them with the basis to make informed business decisions that will allow them to be better equipped in their management and control functions.

In contrast to financial accountancy information, _____ information is:

   - usually confidential and used by management, instead of publicly reported;
   - forward-looking, instead of historical;
   - pragmatically computed using extensive management information systems and internal controls, instead of complying with accounting standards.

This is because of the different emphasis: _____ information is used within an organization, typically for decision-making.

Chapter 1. Management Accounting and Corporate Governance

   a. Governmental accounting
   b. Grenzplankostenrechnung
   c. Nonassurance services
   d. Management accounting

4. A _____ is a fungible, negotiable instrument representing financial value. they are broadly categorized into debt securities (such as banknotes, bonds and debentures), and equity securities; e.g., common stocks. The company or other entity issuing the _____ is called the issuer.
   a. Tracking stock
   b. BMC Software, Inc.
   c. Security
   d. 3M Company

5. The U.S. _____ is an independent agency of the United States government which holds primary responsibility for enforcing the federal securities laws and regulating the securities industry, the nation's stock and options exchanges, and other electronic securities markets. The SEC was created by section 4 of the Securities Exchange Act of 1934 (now codified as 15 U.S.C. §§ 78d and commonly referred to as the 1934 Act.)
   a. 3M Company
   b. Securities and Exchange Commission
   c. BNSF Railway
   d. BMC Software, Inc.

6. _____ is a pricing method used by companies. It is used primarily because it is easy to calculate and requires little information. There are several varieties, but the common thread in all of them is that one first calculates the cost of the product, then includes an additional amount to represent profit.
   a. Cost-plus pricing
   b. Target costing
   c. Price discrimination
   d. Penetration pricing

7. _____ is one of the four Ps of the marketing mix. The other three aspects are product, promotion, and place. It is also a key variable in microeconomic price allocation theory.
   a. Pricing
   b. Price
   c. Target costing
   d. Cost-plus pricing

8. _____ refers to the additional value of a commodity over the cost of commodities used to produce it from the previous stage of production. An example is the price of gasoline at the pump over the price of the oil in it. In national accounts used in macroeconomics, it refers to the contribution of the factors of production, i.e., land, labor, and capital goods, to raising the value of a product and corresponds to the incomes received by the owners of these factors.
   a. Minimum wage
   b. 3M Company
   c. Value added
   d. Supply-side economics

9. In economics, business, retail, and accounting, a _____ is the value of money that has been used up to produce something, and hence is not available for use anymore. In economics, a _____ is an alternative that is given up as a result of a decision. In business, the _____ may be one of acquisition, in which case the amount of money expended to acquire it is counted as _____.
   a. Prime cost
   b. Cost of quality
   c. Cost allocation
   d. Cost

10. A _____ is a fixed point of time in the future at which point certain processes will be evaluated or assumed to end. It is necessary in an accounting, finance or risk management regime to assign such a fixed horizon time so that alternatives can be evaluated for performance over the same period of time. A _____ is a physical impossibility in the real world.
    a. BNSF Railway
    b. BMC Software, Inc.
    c. Time horizon
    d. 3M Company

11. Under the average-cost method, it is assumed that the cost of inventory is based on the _____ of the goods available for sale during the period. _____ is computed by dividing the total cost of goods available for sale by the total units available for sale. This gives a weighted-average unit cost that is applied to the units in the ending inventory.
    a. AIG
    b. ABC Television Network
    c. Ending inventory
    d. Average cost

4 *Chapter 1. Management Accounting and Corporate Governance*

12. _____ is the balance of the amounts of cash being received and paid by a business during a defined period of time, sometimes tied to a specific project. Measurement of _____ can be used

- to evaluate the state or performance of a business or project.
- to determine problems with liquidity. Being profitable does not necessarily mean being liquid. A company can fail because of a shortage of cash, even while profitable.
- to project rate of returns. The time of _____s into and out of projects are used as inputs to financial models such as internal rate of return, and net present value.
- to examine income or growth of a business when it is believed that accrual accounting concepts do not represent economic realities. Alternately, _____ can be used to 'validate' the net income generated by accrual accounting.

_____ as a generic term may be used differently depending on context, and certain _____ definitions may be adapted by analysts and users for their own uses. Common terms include operating _____ and free _____.

a. Commercial paper
b. Controlling interest
c. Flow-through entity
d. Cash flow

13. _____s are goods that have completed the manufacturing process but have not yet been sold or distributed to the end user.

Manufacturing has three classes of inventory:

1. Raw material
2. Work in process
3. _____s

A good purchased as a 'raw material' goes into the manufacture of a product. A good only partially completed during the manufacturing process is called 'work in process'. When the good is completed as to manufacturing but not yet sold or distributed to the end-user is called a '_____'.

a. Reorder point
b. 3M Company
c. Finished Good
d. FIFO and LIFO accounting

14. In business, _____, Overhead cost or _____ expense refers to an ongoing expense of operating a business. The term _____ is usually used to group expenses that are necessary to the continued functioning of the business, but do not directly generate profits.

Chapter 1. Management Accounting and Corporate Governance

_____ expenses are all costs on the income statement except for direct labor and direct materials.

a. Intangible assets
b. AIG
c. ABC Television Network
d. Overhead

15. In business and accounting, _____ are everything of value that is owned by a person or company. It is a claim on the property your income of a borrower. The balance sheet of a firm records the monetary value of the _____ owned by the firm.

a. Accounts receivable
b. Accrual basis accounting
c. Assets
d. Earnings before interest, taxes, depreciation and amortization

16. In accounting, _____ has a very specific meaning. It is an outflow of cash or other valuable assets from a person or company to another person or company. This outflow of cash is generally one side of a trade for products or services that have equal or better current or future value to the buyer than to the seller.

a. AMEX
b. AIG
c. ABC Television Network
d. Expense

17. In financial accounting, a _____ is defined as an obligation of an entity arising from past transactions or events, the settlement of which may result in the transfer or use of assets, provision of services or other yielding of economic benefits in the future.

a. Vested
b. Liability
c. False Claims Act
d. Corporate governance

18. In economic models, the _____ time frame assumes no fixed factors of production. Firms can enter or leave the marketplace, and the cost (and availability) of land, labor, raw materials, and capital goods can be assumed to vary. In contrast, in the short-run time frame, certain factors are assumed to be fixed, because there is not sufficient time for them to change.

a. BMC Software, Inc.
b. Long-run
c. Short-run
d. 3M Company

19. _____ are liabilities with a future benefit over one year, such as notes payable that mature greater than one year.

In accounting, the _____ are shown on the right wing of the balance-sheet representing the sources of funds, which are generally bounded in form of capital assets.

Examples of _____ are debentures, mortgage loans and other bank loans (note: not all bank loans are long term as not all are paid over a period greater than a year, the example is bridging loan.)

a. Long-term liabilities
b. Gross sales
c. Cash basis accounting
d. Book value

20. _____ are formal records of a business' financial activities.

In British English, including United Kingdom company law, _____ are often referred to as accounts, although the term _____ is also used, particularly by accountants.

_____ provide an overview of a business' financial condition in both short and long term.

a. 3M Company
b. Notes to the financial statements
c. Statement of retained earnings
d. Financial statements

21. A _____ is something that is acted upon or used by or by human labour or industry, for use as a building material to create some product or structure. Often the term is used to denote material that came from nature and is in an unprocessed or minimally processed state. Iron ore, logs, and crude oil, would be examples.
a. BMC Software, Inc.
b. BNSF Railway
c. Raw material
d. 3M Company

Chapter 1. Management Accounting and Corporate Governance

22. A _____ is the transfer of wealth from one party (such as a person or company) to another. A _____ is usually made in exchange for the provision of goods, services or both, or to fulfill a legal obligation.

The simplest and oldest form of _____ is barter, the exchange of one good or service for another.

   a. BMC Software, Inc.
   b. Payee
   c. 3M Company
   d. Payment

23. _____ is a process of attributing cost to particular cost centres. For example the wage of the driver of the purchasing department can be allocated to the purchasing department cost centre. It is not necessary to share the wage cost over several different cost centers.
   a. Variable cost
   b. Cost allocation
   c. Cost of quality
   d. Cost accounting

24. _____ are costs that are not directly accountable to a particular function or product. _____ may be either fixed or variable. _____ include taxes, administration, personnel and security costs, and are also known as overhead.
   a. Activity-based costing
   b. ABC Television Network
   c. Indirect costs
   d. Activity-based management

25. _____ refers to the methods, practices and operations conducted to promote and sustain certain categories of commercial activity. The term is understood to have different specific meanings depending on the context. Merchandise is a sale goods at a store

In marketing, one of the definitions of _____ is the practice in which the brand or image from one product or service is used to sell another.

   a. BMC Software, Inc.
   b. Merchandise
   c. 3M Company
   d. Merchandising

Chapter 1. Management Accounting and Corporate Governance

26. Just in Time could refer to the following:

- _____, an inventory strategy that reduces in-process inventory
- _____ compilation, a technique for improving the performance of bytecode-compiled programming systems

a. Comparable
b. Just-in-time
c. Help desk and incident reporting auditing
d. Fiscal

27. _____ is the set of processes, customs, policies, laws, and institutions affecting the way a corporation is directed, administered or controlled. _____ also includes the relationships among the many stakeholders involved and the goals for which the corporation is governed. The principal stakeholders are the shareholders/members, management, and the board of directors.

a. Trust indenture
b. Corporate governance
c. FLSA
d. Patent

28. _____ or economic opportunity loss is the value of the next best alternative foregone as the result of making a decision. _____ analysis is an important part of a company's decision-making processes but is not treated as an actual cost in any financial statement. The next best thing that a person can engage in is referred to as the _____ of doing the best thing and ignoring the next best thing to be done.

a. AIG
b. ABC Television Network
c. Inflation
d. Opportunity cost

29. An _____ is a practitioner of accountancy, which is the measurement, disclosure or provision of assurance about financial information that helps managers, investors, tax authorities and other decision makers make resource allocation decisions.

The word '_____' is derived from the French 'Compter' which took its origin from the Latin 'Computare'. The word was formerly written in English as 'Accomptant', but in process of time the word, which was always pronounced by dropping the 'p', became gradually changed both in pronunciation and in orthography to its present form.

a. AIG
b. AMEX
c. ABC Television Network
d. Accountant

30. The _____ is a professional organization headquartered in Montvale, New Jersey consisting of over 70,000 members worldwide. The IMA is dedicated to advancing the role of the management accountant and financial manager within the business organization, and provides relevant professional certification.

The IMA awards the Certified Management Accountant (CMA) designation in the United States.

a. American Accounting Association
b. International Accounting Standards Committee
c. Institute of Management Accountants
d. Emerging technologies

31. An _____ is a term used in behavioral economics to describe those types of behaviors that impose costs on a person in the long-run that are not taken into account when making decisions in the present. Classical Economics discourages government from creating legislation that targets internalities, because it is assumed that the consumer takes these personal costs into account when paying for the good that causes the _____. For example, cigarettes should be taxed because of the negative consumption externalities that they impose, such as second-hand smoke, not because the smoker harms him or herself by smoking.

a. Inventory turnover ratio
b. Internality
c. Operating budget
d. Authorised capital

32. In accounting and organizational theory, _____ is defined as a process effected by an organization's structure, work and authority flows, people and management information systems, designed to help the organization accomplish specific goals or objectives. It is a means by which an organization's resources are directed, monitored, and measured. It plays an important role in preventing and detecting fraud and protecting the organization's resources, both physical (e.g., machinery and property) and intangible (e.g., reputation or intellectual property such as trademarks.)

a. Internal control
b. Auditor independence
c. Audit risk
d. Audit committee

Chapter 1. Management Accounting and Corporate Governance

33. The _____ of 2002 (Pub.L. 107-204, 116 Stat. 745, enacted July 30, 2002), also known as the Public Company Accounting Reform and Investor Protection Act of 2002, is a United States federal law enacted on July 30, 2002 in response to a number of major corporate and accounting scandals including those affecting Enron, Tyco International, Adelphia, Peregrine Systems and WorldCom. The legislation establishes new or enhanced standards for all U.S. public company boards, management, and public accounting firms. It does not apply to privately held companies.
    a. Sarbanes-Oxley Act
    b. Fair Labor Standards Act
    c. Lease
    d. FCPA

34. In financial accounting, a _____ or Statement of cash flows is a financial statement that shows a company's flow of cash. The money coming into the business is called cash inflow, and money going out from the business is called cash outflow. The statement shows how changes in balance sheet and income accounts affect cash and cash equivalents, and breaks the analysis down to operating, investing, and financing activities.
    a. BNSF Railway
    b. BMC Software, Inc.
    c. 3M Company
    d. Cash flow statement

35. _____ is a method of identifying and evaluating activities that a business performs using activity-based costing to carry out a value chain analysis or a re-engineering initiative to improve strategic and operational decisions in an organization. Activity-based costing establishes relationships between overhead costs and activities so that overhead costs can be more precisely allocated to products, services, or customer segments. _____ focuses on managing activities to reduce costs and improve customer value.
    a. Indirect costs
    b. Activity-based management
    c. ABC Television Network
    d. Activity-based costing

36. _____ is the process of comparing the cost, cycle time, productivity, or quality of a specific process or method to another that is widely considered to be an industry standard or best practice. Essentially, _____ provides a snapshot of the performance of your business and helps you understand where you are in relation to a particular standard. The result is often a business case for making changes in order to make improvements.
    a. Strategic business unit
    b. Benchmarking
    c. BMC Software, Inc.
    d. 3M Company

Chapter 1. Management Accounting and Corporate Governance

37. _____ asserts that there is a technique, method, process, activity, incentive or reward that is more effective at delivering a particular outcome than any other technique, method, process, etc. The idea is that with proper processes, checks, and testing, a desired outcome can be delivered with fewer problems and unforeseen complications. _____s can also be defined as the most efficient (least amount of effort) and effective (best results) way of accomplishing a task, based on repeatable procedures that have proven themselves over time for large numbers of people.

a. Performance measurement
b. Cash cow
c. Management by objectives
d. Best practice

38. _____ Process Deming saw it as part of the 'system' whereby feedback from the process and customer were evaluated against organisational goals.

a. Sole proprietorship
b. Sensitivity analysis
c. Continuous improvement
d. Procurement

39. A _____, also client, buyer or purchaser is the buyer or user of the paid products of an individual or organization, mostly called the supplier or seller. This is typically through purchasing or renting goods or services.

a. 3M Company
b. Customer
c. BNSF Railway
d. BMC Software, Inc.

40. _____, a business term, is a measure of how products and services supplied by a company meet or surpass customer expectation. It is seen as a key performance indicator within business and is part of the four perspectives of a Balanced Scorecard.

In a competitive marketplace where businesses compete for customers, _____ is seen as a key differentiator and increasingly has become a key element of business strategy.

a. Time to market
b. Pre-determined overhead rate
c. Procurement
d. Customer satisfaction

41. _____ is a business management strategy aimed at embedding awareness of quality in all organizational processes. _____ has been widely used in manufacturing, education, call centers, government, and service industries, as well as NASA space and science programs.

When used together as a phrase, the three words in this expression have the following meanings:

- Total: Involving the entire organization, supply chain, and/or product life cycle
- Quality: With its usual definitions, with all its complexities
- Management: The system of managing with steps like Plan, Organize, Control, Lead, Staff, provisioning and organizing.

As defined by the International Organization for Standardization (ISO):

'_____ is a management approach for an organization, centered on quality, based on the participation of all its members and aiming at long-term success through customer satisfaction, and benefits to all members of the organization and to society.' ISO 8402:1994

One major aim is to reduce variation from every process so that greater consistency of effort is obtained. (Royse, D., Thyer, B., Padgett D., ' Logan T., 2006)

In Japan, _____ comprises four process steps, namely:

1. Kaizen - Focuses on 'Continuous Process Improvement', to make processes visible, repeatable and measurable.
2. Atarimae Hinshitsu - The idea that 'things will work as they are supposed to' .
3. Kansei - Examining the way the user applies the product leads to improvement in the product itself.
4. Miryokuteki Hinshitsu - The idea that 'things should have an aesthetic quality' (for example, a pen will write in a way that is pleasing to the writer.)

_____ requires that the company maintain this quality standard in all aspects of its business. This requires ensuring that things are done right the first time and that defects and waste are eliminated from operations.

a. 3M Company
b. Total quality management
c. BMC Software, Inc.
d. BNSF Railway

42. The _____ is a concept from business management that was first described and popularized by Michael Porter in his 1985 best-seller, Competitive Advantage: Creating and Sustaining Superior Performance.

A _____ is a chain of activities. Products pass through all activities of the chain in order and at each activity the product gains some value.

a. Product differentiation
b. Market segmentation
c. Customer relationship management
d. Value chain

43. '_____' is Step 7 of 'Philip Crosby's 14 Step Quality Improvement Process' . Although applicable to any type of enterprise, it has been primarily adopted within industry supply chains wherever large volumes of components are being purchased (common items such as nuts and bolts are good examples.)

_____ was a quality control program originated by the Denver Division of the Martin Marietta Corporation (now Lockheed Martin) on the Titan Missile program, which carried the first astronauts into space in the late 1960s.

a. BMC Software, Inc.
b. BNSF Railway
c. 3M Company
d. Zero defects

44. The term '_____' refers to the concept of collecting information and attempting to spot a pattern in the information. In some fields of study, the term '_____' has more formally-defined meanings.

In project management _____ is a mathematical technique that uses historical results to predict future outcome.

a. Multicollinearity
b. 3M Company
c. Trend analysis
d. Regression analysis

Chapter 2. Cost Behavior, Operating Leverage, and Profitability Analysis

1. _____s are expenses that change in proportion to the activity of a business. In other words, _____ is the sum of marginal costs. It can also be considered normal costs.
   a. Fixed costs
   b. Quality costs
   c. Cost accounting
   d. Variable cost

2. In economics, business, retail, and accounting, a _____ is the value of money that has been used up to produce something, and hence is not available for use anymore. In economics, a _____ is an alternative that is given up as a result of a decision. In business, the _____ may be one of acquisition, in which case the amount of money expended to acquire it is counted as _____.
   a. Cost
   b. Prime cost
   c. Cost of quality
   d. Cost allocation

3. In economics, _____ are business expenses that are not dependent on the activities of the business They tend to be time-related, such as salaries or rents being paid per month. This is in contrast to variable costs, which are volume-related (and are paid per quantity.)

   In management accounting, _____ are defined as expenses that do not change in proportion to the activity of a business, within the relevant period or scale of production.

   a. Cost of quality
   b. Cost accounting
   c. Fixed costs
   d. Marginal cost

4. The _____ is a measure of how revenue growth translates into growth in operating income. It is a measure of leverage, and of how risky (volatile) a company's operating income is.

   There are various measures of _____, which can be interpreted analogously to financial leverage.

   a. Upside potential ratio
   b. Information ratio
   c. AlphaIC
   d. Operating leverage

Chapter 2. Cost Behavior, Operating Leverage, and Profitability Analysis

5. _____ is the balance of the amounts of cash being received and paid by a business during a defined period of time, sometimes tied to a specific project. Measurement of _____ can be used

   - to evaluate the state or performance of a business or project.
   - to determine problems with liquidity. Being profitable does not necessarily mean being liquid. A company can fail because of a shortage of cash, even while profitable.
   - to project rate of returns. The time of _____s into and out of projects are used as inputs to financial models such as internal rate of return, and net present value.
   - to examine income or growth of a business when it is believed that accrual accounting concepts do not represent economic realities. Alternately, _____ can be used to 'validate' the net income generated by accrual accounting.

   _____ as a generic term may be used differently depending on context, and certain _____ definitions may be adapted by analysts and users for their own uses. Common terms include operating _____ and free _____.

   a. Flow-through entity
   b. Cash flow
   c. Controlling interest
   d. Commercial paper

6. In cost-volume-profit analysis, a form of management accounting, _____ is the marginal profit per unit sale. It is a useful quantity in carrying out various calculations, and can be used as a measure of operating leverage.

   The Total _____ is Total Revenue (TR, or Sales) minus Total Variable Cost (TVC):

   Tcontribution margin = TR − TVC

   The Unit _____ (C) is Unit Revenue (Price, P) minus Unit Variable Cost (V):

   C = P − V

   The _____ Ratio is the percentage of Contribution over Total Revenue, which can be calculated from the unit contribution over unit price or total contribution over Total Revenue:

   $$\frac{C}{P} = \frac{P-V}{P} = \frac{\text{Unit Contribution Margin}}{\text{Price}} = \frac{\text{Total Contribution Margin}}{\text{Total Revenue}}$$

   For instance, if the price is $10 and the unit variable cost is $2, then the unit _____ is $8, and the _____ ratio is $8/$10 = 80%.

a. Factory overhead
b. Profit center
c. Cost management
d. Contribution margin

7. _____ is a company's financial statement that indicates how the revenue is transformed into the net income The purpose of the _____ is to show managers and investors whether the company made or lost money during the period being reported.

The important thing to remember about an _____ is that it represents a period of time.

a. AMEX
b. AIG
c. ABC Television Network
d. Income statement

8. In finance, _____ also known as return on investment, rate of profit or sometimes just return, is the ratio of money gained or lost on an investment relative to the amount of money invested. The amount of money gained or lost may be referred to as interest, profit/loss, gain/loss, or net income/loss. The money invested may be referred to as the asset, capital, principal, or the cost basis of the investment.

a. Debt to capital ratio
b. Rate of return
c. Theoretical ex-rights price
d. Capital employed

9. _____ is the calculated approximation of a result which is usable even if input data may be incomplete or uncertain.

In statistics, see _____ theory, estimator.

In mathematics, approximation or _____ typically means finding upper or lower bounds of a quantity that cannot readily be computed precisely and is also an educated guess.

a. AMEX
b. ABC Television Network
c. AIG
d. Estimation

Chapter 2. Cost Behavior, Operating Leverage, and Profitability Analysis

10. A _____ is the transfer of wealth from one party (such as a person or company) to another. A _____ is usually made in exchange for the provision of goods, services or both, or to fulfill a legal obligation.

The simplest and oldest form of _____ is barter, the exchange of one good or service for another.

a. 3M Company
b. BMC Software, Inc.
c. Payee
d. Payment

11. _____ is an area of engineering practice concerned with the 'application of scientific principles and techniques to problems of cost estimating, cost control, business planning and management science, profitability analysis, project management, and planning and scheduling.'

Key objectives of _____ are to arrive at accurate cost estimates and to avoid cost overruns. The broad array of _____ topics represent the intersection of the fields of project management, business management, and engineering. Most people have a limited view of what engineering encompasses.

a. BNSF Railway
b. BMC Software, Inc.
c. 3M Company
d. Cost engineering

Chapter 3. Analysis of Cost, Volume, and Pricing to Increase Profitability

1. _____, in managerial economics is a form of cost accounting. It is a simplified model, useful for elementary instruction and for short-run decisions.

Cost-volume-profit (CVP) analysis expands the use of information provided by breakeven analysis.

a. Cost of quality
b. Fixed costs
c. Cost accounting
d. Cost-volume-profit analysis

2. In economics ' business, specifically cost accounting, the _____ is the point at which cost or expenses and revenue are equal: there is no net loss or gain, and one has 'broken even'. A profit or a loss has not been made, although opportunity costs have been paid, and capital has received the risk-adjusted, expected return.

For example, if the business sells less than 200 tables each month, it will make a loss, if it sells more, it will be a profit.

a. BMC Software, Inc.
b. Defined benefit pension plan
c. Break-even point
d. 3M Company

3. In cost-volume-profit analysis, a form of management accounting, _____ is the marginal profit per unit sale. It is a useful quantity in carrying out various calculations, and can be used as a measure of operating leverage.

The Total _____ is Total Revenue (TR, or Sales) minus Total Variable Cost (TVC):

Tcontribution margin = TR − TVC

The Unit _____ (C) is Unit Revenue (Price, P) minus Unit Variable Cost (V):

C = P − V

The _____ Ratio is the percentage of Contribution over Total Revenue, which can be calculated from the unit contribution over unit price or total contribution over Total Revenue:

$$\frac{C}{P} = \frac{P-V}{P} = \frac{\text{Unit Contribution Margin}}{\text{Price}} = \frac{\text{Total Contribution Margin}}{\text{Total Revenue}}$$

For instance, if the price is $10 and the unit variable cost is $2, then the unit _____ is $8, and the _____ ratio is $8/$10 = 80%.

Chapter 3. Analysis of Cost, Volume, and Pricing to Increase Profitability

a. Factory overhead
b. Profit center
c. Contribution margin
d. Cost management

4. A _____ is the pinnacle activity involved in selling products or services in return for money or other compensation. It is an act of completion of a commercial activity.

A _____ is completed by the seller, the owner of the goods.

a. Tertiary sector of economy
b. Maturity
c. High yield stock
d. Sale

5. _____ is a pricing method used by companies. It is used primarily because it is easy to calculate and requires little information. There are several varieties, but the common thread in all of them is that one first calculates the cost of the product, then includes an additional amount to represent profit.

a. Penetration pricing
b. Cost-plus pricing
c. Price discrimination
d. Target costing

6. _____ is one of the four Ps of the marketing mix. The other three aspects are product, promotion, and place. It is also a key variable in microeconomic price allocation theory.

a. Price
b. Target costing
c. Cost-plus pricing
d. Pricing

7. _____ is a pricing method used by firms. It is defined as 'a cost management tool for reducing the overall cost of a product over its entire life-cycle with the help of production, engineering, research and design'. A target cost is the maximum amount of cost that can be incurred on a product and with it the firm can still earn the required profit margin from that product at a particular selling price.

a. Target costing
b. Penetration pricing
c. Discounts and allowances
d. Pricing

8. _____ is a costing model that identifies activities in an organization and assigns the cost of each activity resource to all products and services according to the actual consumption by each: it assigns more indirect costs (overhead) into direct costs.

In this way an organization can establish the true cost of its individual products and services for the purposes of identifying and eliminating those which are unprofitable and lowering the prices of those which are overpriced.

In a business organization, the ABC methodology assigns an organization's resource costs through activities to the products and services provided to its customers.

a. Indirect costs
b. Activity-based management
c. Activity-based Costing
d. ABC Television Network

9. _____ refers to the pricing of contributions (assets, tangible and intangible, services, and funds) transferred within an organization. For example, goods from the production division may be sold to the marketing division, or goods from a parent company may be sold to a foreign subsidiary. Since the prices are set within an organization (i.e. controlled), the typical market mechanisms that establish prices for such transactions between third parties may not apply.

a. Pricing
b. Transactional Net Margin Method
c. Price
d. Transfer Pricing

10. _____s are expenses that change in proportion to the activity of a business. In other words, _____ is the sum of marginal costs. It can also be considered normal costs.

a. Variable cost
b. Cost accounting
c. Fixed costs
d. Quality costs

Chapter 3. Analysis of Cost, Volume, and Pricing to Increase Profitability   21

11. In economics, business, retail, and accounting, a _____ is the value of money that has been used up to produce something, and hence is not available for use anymore. In economics, a _____ is an alternative that is given up as a result of a decision. In business, the _____ may be one of acquisition, in which case the amount of money expended to acquire it is counted as _____.

   a. Cost
   b. Cost of quality
   c. Prime cost
   d. Cost allocation

12. A _____ is the transfer of wealth from one party (such as a person or company) to another. A _____ is usually made in exchange for the provision of goods, services or both, or to fulfill a legal obligation.

The simplest and oldest form of _____ is barter, the exchange of one good or service for another.

   a. Payee
   b. BMC Software, Inc.
   c. 3M Company
   d. Payment

13. _____ is the balance of the amounts of cash being received and paid by a business during a defined period of time, sometimes tied to a specific project. Measurement of _____ can be used

   - to evaluate the state or performance of a business or project.
   - to determine problems with liquidity. Being profitable does not necessarily mean being liquid. A company can fail because of a shortage of cash, even while profitable.
   - to project rate of returns. The time of _____s into and out of projects are used as inputs to financial models such as internal rate of return, and net present value.
   - to examine income or growth of a business when it is believed that accrual accounting concepts do not represent economic realities. Alternately, _____ can be used to 'validate' the net income generated by accrual accounting.

_____ as a generic term may be used differently depending on context, and certain _____ definitions may be adapted by analysts and users for their own uses. Common terms include operating _____ and free _____.

   a. Commercial paper
   b. Flow-through entity
   c. Controlling interest
   d. Cash flow

Chapter 3. Analysis of Cost, Volume, and Pricing to Increase Profitability

14. In economics, _____ are business expenses that are not dependent on the activities of the business They tend to be time-related, such as salaries or rents being paid per month. This is in contrast to variable costs, which are volume-related (and are paid per quantity.)

In management accounting, _____ are defined as expenses that do not change in proportion to the activity of a business, within the relevant period or scale of production.

   a. Cost of quality
   b. Cost accounting
   c. Marginal cost
   d. Fixed costs

15. _____ is the study of how the variation (uncertainty) in the output of a mathematical model can be apportioned, qualitatively or quantitatively, to different sources of variation in the input of a model .

In more general terms uncertainty and sensitivity analyses investigate the robustness of a study when the study includes some form of mathematical modelling. While uncertainty analysis studies the overall uncertainty in the conclusions of the study, _____ tries to identify what source of uncertainty weights more on the study's conclusions.

   a. Free cash flow
   b. Time to market
   c. Kaizen
   d. Sensitivity analysis

16. A _____ is a computer application that simulates a paper worksheet. It displays multiple cells that together make up a grid consisting of rows and columns, each cell containing either alphanumeric text or numeric values. A _____ cell may alternatively contain a formula that defines how the contents of that cell is to be calculated from the contents of any other cell (or combination of cells) each time any cell is updated.
   a. Mutual fund
   b. Merck ' Co., Inc.
   c. Linear regression
   d. Spreadsheet

17. _____ in economics and business is the result of an exchange and from that trade we assign a numerical monetary value to a good, service or asset. If Alice trades Bob 4 apples for an orange, the _____ of an orange is 4 apples. Inversely, the _____ of an apple is 1/4 oranges.

a. Transactional Net Margin Method
b. Price
c. Price discrimination
d. Discounts and allowances

18. _____ is the collection, transport, processing, recycling or disposal, and monitoring of waste materials. The term usually relates to materials produced by human activity, and is generally undertaken to reduce their effect on health, the environment or aesthetics. _____ is also carried out to recover resources from it.
a. BMC Software, Inc.
b. 3M Company
c. BNSF Railway
d. Waste Management

1. In economics, business, retail, and accounting, a _____ is the value of money that has been used up to produce something, and hence is not available for use anymore. In economics, a _____ is an alternative that is given up as a result of a decision. In business, the _____ may be one of acquisition, in which case the amount of money expended to acquire it is counted as _____.
   a. Prime cost
   b. Cost allocation
   c. Cost
   d. Cost of quality

2. A _____ is a tangible input for a product manufactured/Service provided, like labor or material. For example a cloth manufacturing firm requires some amount of predetermined labor and predetermined raw material for any amount of cloth being manufactured. The cost of employing labor can be directly fixed as 'per man per hour' or 'per man per day', so the labor is a _____ as you can directly associate cost with it.
   a. Round-tripping
   b. Cost object
   c. Residual value
   d. 3M Company

3. A '_____' is the unit of an activity that causes the change of an activity cost. A _____ is any activity that causes a cost to be incurred. The Activity Based Costing (ABC) approach relates indirect cost to the activities that drive them to be incurred.
   a. Contribution margin analysis
   b. Cost driver
   c. Profit center
   d. Factory overhead

4. _____ consists of the sale of goods or merchandise from a fixed location, such as a department store, boutique or kiosk in small or individual lots for direct consumption by the purchaser. _____ may include subordinated services, such as delivery. Purchasers may be individuals or businesses.
   a. 3M Company
   b. BMC Software, Inc.
   c. BNSF Railway
   d. Retailing

5. _____ is a process of attributing cost to particular cost centres. For example the wage of the driver of the purchasing department can be allocated to the purchasing department cost centre. It is not necessary to share the wage cost over several different cost centers.

a. Variable cost
b. Cost accounting
c. Cost of quality
d. Cost allocation

6. _____s are expenses that change in proportion to the activity of a business. In other words, _____ is the sum of marginal costs. It can also be considered normal costs.
a. Quality costs
b. Cost accounting
c. Variable cost
d. Fixed costs

7. _____ are costs that are not directly accountable to a particular function or product. _____ may be either fixed or variable. _____ include taxes, administration, personnel and security costs, and are also known as overhead.
a. Activity-based management
b. ABC Television Network
c. Activity-based costing
d. Indirect costs

8. A _____ is the transfer of wealth from one party (such as a person or company) to another. A _____ is usually made in exchange for the provision of goods, services or both, or to fulfill a legal obligation.

The simplest and oldest form of _____ is barter, the exchange of one good or service for another.

a. BMC Software, Inc.
b. Payment
c. Payee
d. 3M Company

9. _____, in managerial economics is a form of cost accounting. It is a simplified model, useful for elementary instruction and for short-run decisions.

Cost-volume-profit (CVP) analysis expands the use of information provided by breakeven analysis.

a. Cost-volume-profit analysis
b. Cost accounting
c. Fixed costs
d. Cost of quality

10. In business, _____, Overhead cost or _____ expense refers to an ongoing expense of operating a business. The term _____ is usually used to group expenses that are necessary to the continued functioning of the business, but do not directly generate profits.

_____ expenses are all costs on the income statement except for direct labor and direct materials.

a. Intangible assets
b. AIG
c. Overhead
d. ABC Television Network

11. In economics, _____ are business expenses that are not dependent on the activities of the business They tend to be time-related, such as salaries or rents being paid per month. This is in contrast to variable costs, which are volume-related (and are paid per quantity.)

In management accounting, _____ are defined as expenses that do not change in proportion to the activity of a business, within the relevant period or scale of production.

a. Marginal cost
b. Cost accounting
c. Cost of quality
d. Fixed costs

12. A _____ is the rate used to apply manufacturing overhead to work-in-process inventory. It is calculated as estimated manufacturing overhead cost divided by estimated amount of cost driver or activity base. Common activity bases used in the calculation include direct labor costs, direct labor hours, or machine hours.
a. Procurement
b. Kaizen
c. Pre-determined overhead rate
d. Sensitivity analysis

13. A _____ is the pinnacle activity involved in selling products or services in return for money or other compensation. It is an act of completion of a commercial activity.

Chapter 4. Cost Accumulation Tracing, and Allocation   27

A _____ is completed by the seller, the owner of the goods.

a. Maturity
b. Tertiary sector of economy
c. High yield stock
d. Sale

14. In mathematics _____s are numbers or other things that get multiplied. In particular, see:

- Factorization, the decomposition of an object into a product of other objects
- Integer factorization, the process of breaking down a composite number into smaller non-trivial divisors
- A coefficient
- A divisor of a particular number, or of an element of a monoid
- A von Neumann algebra with a trivial center

In statistics

- _____ analysis is the study of how _____s or certain variables affect variables.

In technology:

- Human _____s, a profession that focuses on how people interact with products, tools, or procedures
- 'Functionality, Application domain, Conditions, Technology, Objects and Responsibility;', In object-oriented programming

In computer science and information technology:

- Authentication _____, a piece of information used to verify a person's identity for security purposes
- _____, a Unix command for numbers factorization
- _____ (programming language), an experimental Forth-like programming language

In television:

- The O'Reilly _____, an American talk show hosted by Bill O'Reilly on Fox News.
- The Krypton _____, a British game show hosted by Gordon Burns, formally on ITV. Also had an American version.

a. Valuation
b. Merck ' Co., Inc.
c. Factor
d. The Goodyear Tire ' Rubber Company

Chapter 5. Relevant Information for Special Decisions

1. In economics and business decision-making, _____ are costs that cannot be recovered once they have been incurred. _____ are sometimes contrasted with variable costs, which are the costs that will change due to the proposed course of action, and prospective costs which are costs that will be incurred if an action is taken.

In traditional microeconomic theory, only variable costs are relevant to a decision.

   a. 3M Company
   b. BNSF Railway
   c. BMC Software, Inc.
   d. Sunk costs

2. In economics, business, retail, and accounting, a _____ is the value of money that has been used up to produce something, and hence is not available for use anymore. In economics, a _____ is an alternative that is given up as a result of a decision. In business, the _____ may be one of acquisition, in which case the amount of money expended to acquire it is counted as _____.

   a. Cost allocation
   b. Cost of quality
   c. Prime cost
   d. Cost

3. A _____ is the transfer of wealth from one party (such as a person or company) to another. A _____ is usually made in exchange for the provision of goods, services or both, or to fulfill a legal obligation.

The simplest and oldest form of _____ is barter, the exchange of one good or service for another.

   a. Payment
   b. 3M Company
   c. BMC Software, Inc.
   d. Payee

4. _____ or economic opportunity loss is the value of the next best alternative foregone as the result of making a decision. _____ analysis is an important part of a company's decision-making processes but is not treated as an actual cost in any financial statement. The next best thing that a person can engage in is referred to as the _____ of doing the best thing and ignoring the next best thing to be done.

   a. Inflation
   b. AIG
   c. ABC Television Network
   d. Opportunity cost

Chapter 5. Relevant Information for Special Decisions

5. _____ is the balance of the amounts of cash being received and paid by a business during a defined period of time, sometimes tied to a specific project. Measurement of _____ can be used

- to evaluate the state or performance of a business or project.
- to determine problems with liquidity. Being profitable does not necessarily mean being liquid. A company can fail because of a shortage of cash, even while profitable.
- to project rate of returns. The time of _____s into and out of projects are used as inputs to financial models such as internal rate of return, and net present value.
- to examine income or growth of a business when it is believed that accrual accounting concepts do not represent economic realities. Alternately, _____ can be used to 'validate' the net income generated by accrual accounting.

_____ as a generic term may be used differently depending on context, and certain _____ definitions may be adapted by analysts and users for their own uses. Common terms include operating _____ and free _____.

a. Cash flow
b. Commercial paper
c. Flow-through entity
d. Controlling interest

6. _____ is subcontracting a process, such as product design or manufacturing, to a third-party company. The decision to outsource is often made in the interest of lowering cost or making better use of time and energy costs, redirecting or conserving energy directed at the competencies of a particular business, or to make more efficient use of land, labor, capital, (information) technology and resources. _____ became part of the business lexicon during the 1980s.
a. US Airways, Inc.
b. Economic Growth and Tax Relief Reconciliation Act of 2001
c. USA Today
d. Outsourcing

7. In mathematics _____s are numbers or other things that get multiplied. In particular, see:

- Factorization, the decomposition of an object into a product of other objects
- Integer factorization, the process of breaking down a composite number into smaller non-trivial divisors
- A coefficient
- A divisor of a particular number, or of an element of a monoid
- A von Neumann algebra with a trivial center

In statistics

- _____ analysis is the study of how _____s or certain variables affect variables.

Chapter 5. Relevant Information for Special Decisions

In technology:

- Human _____s, a profession that focuses on how people interact with products, tools, or procedures
- 'Functionality, Application domain, Conditions, Technology, Objects and Responsibility;', In object-oriented programming

In computer science and information technology:

- Authentication _____, a piece of information used to verify a person's identity for security purposes
- _____, a Unix command for numbers factorization
- _____ (programming language), an experimental Forth-like programming language

In television:

- The O'Reilly _____, an American talk show hosted by Bill O'Reilly on Fox News.
- The Krypton _____, a British game show hosted by Gordon Burns, formally on ITV. Also had an American version.

a. Factor
b. The Goodyear Tire ' Rubber Company
c. Valuation
d. Merck ' Co., Inc.

8. _____ is one of the four Ps of the marketing mix. The other three aspects are product, promotion, and place. It is also a key variable in microeconomic price allocation theory.
   a. Price
   b. Target costing
   c. Pricing
   d. Cost-plus pricing

9. In microeconomics and management, the term _____ describes a style of management control. Vertically integrated companies are united through a hierarchy with a common owner. Usually each member of the hierarchy produces a different product or (market-specific) service, and the products combine to satisfy a common need.
   a. 3M Company
   b. Vertical integration
   c. BMC Software, Inc.
   d. BNSF Railway

Chapter 6. Cost Management in an Automated Business Environment: ABC, ABM, and TQM

1. In economics, business, retail, and accounting, a _____ is the value of money that has been used up to produce something, and hence is not available for use anymore. In economics, a _____ is an alternative that is given up as a result of a decision. In business, the _____ may be one of acquisition, in which case the amount of money expended to acquire it is counted as _____.
   a. Cost of quality
   b. Cost allocation
   c. Prime cost
   d. Cost

2. A '_____' is the unit of an activity that causes the change of an activity cost. A _____ is any activity that causes a cost to be incurred. The Activity Based Costing (ABC) approach relates indirect cost to the activities that drive them to be incurred.
   a. Factory overhead
   b. Profit center
   c. Contribution margin analysis
   d. Cost driver

3. _____ is a costing model that identifies activities in an organization and assigns the cost of each activity resource to all products and services according to the actual consumption by each: it assigns more indirect costs (overhead) into direct costs.

   In this way an organization can establish the true cost of its individual products and services for the purposes of identifying and eliminating those which are unprofitable and lowering the prices of those which are overpriced.

   In a business organization, the ABC methodology assigns an organization's resource costs through activities to the products and services provided to its customers.

   a. Activity-based management
   b. Activity-based costing
   c. ABC Television Network
   d. Indirect costs

4. _____ is a process of attributing cost to particular cost centres. For example the wage of the driver of the purchasing department can be allocated to the purchasing department cost centre. It is not necessary to share the wage cost over several different cost centers.
   a. Cost accounting
   b. Variable cost
   c. Cost of quality
   d. Cost allocation

Chapter 6. Cost Management in an Automated Business Environment: ABC, ABM, and TQM

5. _____ is a company's financial statement that indicates how the revenue is transformed into the net income The purpose of the _____ is to show managers and investors whether the company made or lost money during the period being reported.

The important thing to remember about an _____ is that it represents a period of time.

a. AMEX
b. AIG
c. ABC Television Network
d. Income statement

6. A _____ rocket is a rocket that uses two or more stages, each of which contains its own engines and propellant. A tandem or serial stage is mounted on top of another stage; a parallel stage is attached alongside another stage. The result is effectively two or more rockets stacked on top of or attached next to each other.

a. BNSF Railway
b. BMC Software, Inc.
c. 3M Company
d. Multistage

7. _____ is a method of identifying and evaluating activities that a business performs using activity-based costing to carry out a value chain analysis or a re-engineering initiative to improve strategic and operational decisions in an organization. Activity-based costing establishes relationships between overhead costs and activities so that overhead costs can be more precisely allocated to products, services, or customer segments. _____ focuses on managing activities to reduce costs and improve customer value.

a. Activity-based costing
b. Activity-based management
c. Indirect costs
d. ABC Television Network

8. _____ is the balance of the amounts of cash being received and paid by a business during a defined period of time, sometimes tied to a specific project. Measurement of _____ can be used

- to evaluate the state or performance of a business or project.
- to determine problems with liquidity. Being profitable does not necessarily mean being liquid. A company can fail because of a shortage of cash, even while profitable.
- to project rate of returns. The time of _____s into and out of projects are used as inputs to financial models such as internal rate of return, and net present value.
- to examine income or growth of a business when it is believed that accrual accounting concepts do not represent economic realities. Alternately, _____ can be used to 'validate' the net income generated by accrual accounting.

Chapter 6. Cost Management in an Automated Business Environment: ABC, ABM, and TQM

_____ as a generic term may be used differently depending on context, and certain _____ definitions may be adapted by analysts and users for their own uses. Common terms include operating _____ and free _____.

a. Controlling interest
b. Cash flow
c. Flow-through entity
d. Commercial paper

9. A _____ is the transfer of wealth from one party (such as a person or company) to another. A _____ is usually made in exchange for the provision of goods, services or both, or to fulfill a legal obligation.

The simplest and oldest form of _____ is barter, the exchange of one good or service for another.

a. Payment
b. Payee
c. BMC Software, Inc.
d. 3M Company

10. _____ is one of the four Ps of the marketing mix. The other three aspects are product, promotion, and place. It is also a key variable in microeconomic price allocation theory.

a. Target costing
b. Cost-plus pricing
c. Pricing
d. Price

11. Employment is a contract between two parties, one being the employer and the other being the _____. An _____ may be defined as: 'A person in the service of another under any contract of hire, express or implied, oral or written, where the employer has the power or right to control and direct the _____ in the material details of how the work is to be performed.' Black's Law Dictionary page 471 (5th ed. 1979.)

a. AMEX
b. AIG
c. ABC Television Network
d. Employee

12. _____ is the process whereby companies use cost accounting to report or control the various costs of doing business.

Chapter 6. Cost Management in an Automated Business Environment: ABC, ABM, and TQM

The term _____ is widely used in business today. Unfortunately _____ has no uniform definition.

a. Contribution margin analysis
b. Cost management
c. Contribution margin
d. Process costing

13. An _____ is a term used in behavioral economics to describe those types of behaviors that impose costs on a person in the long-run that are not taken into account when making decisions in the present. Classical Economics discourages government from creating legislation that targets internalities, because it is assumed that the consumer takes these personal costs into account when paying for the good that causes the _____. For example, cigarettes should be taxed because of the negative consumption externalities that they impose, such as second-hand smoke, not because the smoker harms him or herself by smoking.

a. Authorised capital
b. Internality
c. Operating budget
d. Inventory turnover ratio

14. _____ is a business management strategy aimed at embedding awareness of quality in all organizational processes. _____ has been widely used in manufacturing, education, call centers, government, and service industries, as well as NASA space and science programs.

When used together as a phrase, the three words in this expression have the following meanings:

- Total: Involving the entire organization, supply chain, and/or product life cycle
- Quality: With its usual definitions, with all its complexities
- Management: The system of managing with steps like Plan, Organize, Control, Lead, Staff, provisioning and organizing.

As defined by the International Organization for Standardization (ISO):

'_____ is a management approach for an organization, centered on quality, based on the participation of all its members and aiming at long-term success through customer satisfaction, and benefits to all members of the organization and to society.' ISO 8402:1994

One major aim is to reduce variation from every process so that greater consistency of effort is obtained. (Royse, D., Thyer, B., Padgett D., ' Logan T., 2006)

Chapter 6. Cost Management in an Automated Business Environment: ABC, ABM, and TQM

In Japan, _____ comprises four process steps, namely:

1. Kaizen - Focuses on 'Continuous Process Improvement', to make processes visible, repeatable and measurable.
2. Atarimae Hinshitsu - The idea that 'things will work as they are supposed to'.
3. Kansei - Examining the way the user applies the product leads to improvement in the product itself.
4. Miryokuteki Hinshitsu - The idea that 'things should have an aesthetic quality' (for example, a pen will write in a way that is pleasing to the writer.)

_____ requires that the company maintain this quality standard in all aspects of its business. This requires ensuring that things are done right the first time and that defects and waste are eliminated from operations.

a. 3M Company
b. BMC Software, Inc.
c. Total quality management
d. BNSF Railway

Chapter 7. Planning for Profit and Cost Control

1. In economics, _____ or _____ goods or real _____ refers to factors of production used to create goods or services that are not themselves significantly consumed (though they may depreciate) in the production process. _____ goods may be acquired with money or financial _____. In finance and accounting, _____ generally refers to financial wealth, especially that used to start or maintain a business.

    a. Disclosure
    b. Screening
    c. Capital
    d. Vyborg Appeal

2. _____ is the planning process used to determine whether a firm's long term investments such as new machinery, replacement machinery, new plants, new products, and research development projects are worth pursuing. It is budget for major capital, or investment, expenditures.

    Many formal methods are used in _____, including the techniques such as

    - Net present value
    - Profitability index
    - Internal rate of return
    - Modified Internal Rate of Return
    - Equivalent annuity

    These methods use the incremental cash flows from each potential investment, or project. Techniques based on accounting earnings and accounting rules are sometimes used - though economists consider this to be improper - such as the accounting rate of return, and 'return on investment.' Simplified and hybrid methods are used as well, such as payback period and discounted payback period.

    a. Cash flow
    b. Preferred stock
    c. Gross profit
    d. Capital budgeting

3. _____ is an organization's process of defining its strategy and making decisions on allocating its resources to pursue this strategy, including its capital and people. Various business analysis techniques can be used in _____, including SWOT analysis (Strengths, Weaknesses, Opportunities, and Threats) and PEST analysis (Political, Economic, Social, and Technological analysis) or STEER analysis involving Socio-cultural, Technological, Economic, Ecological, and Regulatory factors and EPISTEL (Environment, Political, Informatic, Social, Technological, Economic and Legal)

Chapter 7. Planning for Profit and Cost Control

_____ is the formal consideration of an organization's future course. All _____ deals with at least one of three key questions:

1. 'What do we do?'
2. 'For whom do we do it?'
3. 'How do we excel?'

In business _____, the third question is better phrased 'How can we beat or avoid competition?'. (Bradford and Duncan, page 1.)

a. BNSF Railway
b. 3M Company
c. Strategic planning
d. BMC Software, Inc.

4. _____ is systematic determination of merit, worth, and significance of something or someone using criteria against a set of standards. _____ often is used to characterize and appraise subjects of interest in a wide range of human enterprises, including the arts, criminal justice, foundations and non-profit organizations, government, health care, and other human services.

Depending on the topic of interest, there are professional groups which look to the quality and rigor of the _____ process.

a. ABC Television Network
b. AMEX
c. AIG
d. Evaluation

5. In probability theory and statistics, the _____ of a random variable, probability distribution averaging the squared distance of its possible values from the expected value (mean.) Whereas the mean is a way to describe the location of a distribution, the _____ is a way to capture its scale or degree of being spread out. The unit of _____ is the square of the unit of the original variable.

a. Variance
b. Time series
c. Statistics
d. Monte Carlo methods

Chapter 7. Planning for Profit and Cost Control

6. An _____ is the annual budget of an activity stated in terms of Budget Classification Code, functional/subfunctional categories and cost accounts. It contains estimates of the total value of resources required for the performance of the operation including reimbursable work or services for others. It also includes estimates of workload in terms of total work units identified by cost accounts.
    a. Internality
    b. Operating budget
    c. Inventory turnover ratio
    d. Authorised capital

7. The term _____ is a term applied to practices that are perfunctory, or seek to satisfy the minimum requirements or to conform to a convention or doctrine. It has different meanings in different fields.

In accounting, _____ earnings are those earnings of companies in addition to actual earnings calculated under the Generally Accepted Accounting Principles (GAAP) in their quarterly and yearly financial reports.

   a. Pro forma
   b. Treasury stock
   c. Bottom line
   d. Payroll

8. Project _____: The project _____ is a prediction of the costs associated with a particular company project. These costs include labor, materials, and other related expenses. The project _____ is often broken down into specific tasks, with task _____s assigned to each.
    a. 3M Company
    b. BNSF Railway
    c. Budget
    d. BMC Software, Inc.

9. In mathematics _____s are numbers or other things that get multiplied. In particular, see:

   - Factorization, the decomposition of an object into a product of other objects
   - Integer factorization, the process of breaking down a composite number into smaller non-trivial divisors
   - A coefficient
   - A divisor of a particular number, or of an element of a monoid
   - A von Neumann algebra with a trivial center

In statistics

   - _____ analysis is the study of how _____s or certain variables affect variables.

In technology:

- Human _____s, a profession that focuses on how people interact with products, tools, or procedures
- 'Functionality, Application domain, Conditions, Technology, Objects and Responsibility;', In object-oriented programming

In computer science and information technology:

- Authentication _____, a piece of information used to verify a person's identity for security purposes
- _____, a Unix command for numbers factorization
- _____ (programming language), an experimental Forth-like programming language

In television:

- The O'Reilly _____, an American talk show hosted by Bill O'Reilly on Fox News.
- The Krypton _____, a British game show hosted by Gordon Burns, formally on ITV. Also had an American version.

a. The Goodyear Tire ' Rubber Company
b. Valuation
c. Merck ' Co., Inc.
d. Factor

10. _____ are formal records of a business' financial activities.

In British English, including United Kingdom company law, _____ are often referred to as accounts, although the term _____ is also used, particularly by accountants.

_____ provide an overview of a business' financial condition in both short and long term.

a. Statement of retained earnings
b. Notes to the financial statements
c. 3M Company
d. Financial statements

11. A _____ is the pinnacle activity involved in selling products or services in return for money or other compensation. It is an act of completion of a commercial activity.

A _____ is completed by the seller, the owner of the goods.

Chapter 7. Planning for Profit and Cost Control

a. High yield stock
b. Maturity
c. Tertiary sector of economy
d. Sale

12. A _____ is the transfer of wealth from one party (such as a person or company) to another. A _____ is usually made in exchange for the provision of goods, services or both, or to fulfill a legal obligation.

The simplest and oldest form of _____ is barter, the exchange of one good or service for another.

a. 3M Company
b. BMC Software, Inc.
c. Payee
d. Payment

13. _____ is the balance of the amounts of cash being received and paid by a business during a defined period of time, sometimes tied to a specific project. Measurement of _____ can be used

- to evaluate the state or performance of a business or project.
- to determine problems with liquidity. Being profitable does not necessarily mean being liquid. A company can fail because of a shortage of cash, even while profitable.
- to project rate of returns. The time of _____s into and out of projects are used as inputs to financial models such as internal rate of return, and net present value.
- to examine income or growth of a business when it is believed that accrual accounting concepts do not represent economic realities. Alternately, _____ can be used to 'validate' the net income generated by accrual accounting.

_____ as a generic term may be used differently depending on context, and certain _____ definitions may be adapted by analysts and users for their own uses. Common terms include operating _____ and free _____.

a. Flow-through entity
b. Controlling interest
c. Commercial paper
d. Cash flow

14. _____ refers to a business or organization attempting to acquire goods or services to accomplish the goals of the enterprise. Though there are several organizations that attempt to set standards in the _____ process, processes can vary greatly between organizations. Typically the word e;_____e; is not used interchangeably with the word e;procuremente;, since procurement typically includes Expediting, Supplier Quality, and Traffic and Logistics (T'L) in addition to _____.

a. Supply chain
b. Consignor
c. Free port
d. Purchasing

15. In accounting, _____ has a very specific meaning. It is an outflow of cash or other valuable assets from a person or company to another person or company. This outflow of cash is generally one side of a trade for products or services that have equal or better current or future value to the buyer than to the seller.
a. ABC Television Network
b. AMEX
c. AIG
d. Expense

16. _____ is a company's financial statement that indicates how the revenue is transformed into the net income The purpose of the _____ is to show managers and investors whether the company made or lost money during the period being reported.

The important thing to remember about an _____ is that it represents a period of time.

a. AIG
b. Income statement
c. ABC Television Network
d. AMEX

17. In financial accounting, a _____ or statement of financial position is a summary of a person's or organization's balances. Assets, liabilities and ownership equity are listed as of a specific date, such as the end of its financial year. A _____ is often described as a snapshot of a company's financial condition.
a. Balance sheet
b. 3M Company
c. Statement of retained earnings
d. Financial statements

Chapter 8. Performance Evaluation

1. _____ is systematic determination of merit, worth, and significance of something or someone using criteria against a set of standards. _____ often is used to characterize and appraise subjects of interest in a wide range of human enterprises, including the arts, criminal justice, foundations and non-profit organizations, government, health care, and other human services.

Depending on the topic of interest, there are professional groups which look to the quality and rigor of the _____ process.

   a. ABC Television Network
   b. AMEX
   c. Evaluation
   d. AIG

2. Project _____: The project _____ is a prediction of the costs associated with a particular company project. These costs include labor, materials, and other related expenses. The project _____ is often broken down into specific tasks, with task _____s assigned to each.
   a. 3M Company
   b. Budget
   c. BMC Software, Inc.
   d. BNSF Railway

3. A _____ is the pinnacle activity involved in selling products or services in return for money or other compensation. It is an act of completion of a commercial activity.

A _____ is completed by the seller, the owner of the goods.

   a. High yield stock
   b. Tertiary sector of economy
   c. Sale
   d. Maturity

4. In probability theory and statistics, the _____ of a random variable, probability distribution averaging the squared distance of its possible values from the expected value (mean.) Whereas the mean is a way to describe the location of a distribution, the _____ is a way to capture its scale or degree of being spread out. The unit of _____ is the square of the unit of the original variable.
   a. Variance
   b. Time series
   c. Monte Carlo methods
   d. Statistics

Chapter 8. Performance Evaluation

5. _____s are expenses that change in proportion to the activity of a business. In other words, _____ is the sum of marginal costs. It can also be considered normal costs.
   a. Fixed costs
   b. Cost accounting
   c. Variable cost
   d. Quality costs

6. In economics, business, retail, and accounting, a _____ is the value of money that has been used up to produce something, and hence is not available for use anymore. In economics, a _____ is an alternative that is given up as a result of a decision. In business, the _____ may be one of acquisition, in which case the amount of money expended to acquire it is counted as _____.
   a. Cost of quality
   b. Cost
   c. Cost allocation
   d. Prime cost

7. In economics, _____ are business expenses that are not dependent on the activities of the business They tend to be time-related, such as salaries or rents being paid per month. This is in contrast to variable costs, which are volume-related (and are paid per quantity.)

   In management accounting, _____ are defined as expenses that do not change in proportion to the activity of a business, within the relevant period or scale of production.

   a. Marginal cost
   b. Cost accounting
   c. Cost of quality
   d. Fixed costs

8. _____ in economics and business is the result of an exchange and from that trade we assign a numerical monetary value to a good, service or asset. If Alice trades Bob 4 apples for an orange, the _____ of an orange is 4 apples. Inversely, the _____ of an apple is 1/4 oranges.
   a. Price discrimination
   b. Transactional Net Margin Method
   c. Price
   d. Discounts and allowances

9. The materials _____ is computed as follows:

Chapter 8. Performance Evaluation

Vmp = (Actual Unit Cost - Standard Unit Cost) * Actual Quantity Purchased

or

Vmp = (Actual Quantity Purchased * Actual Unit Cost) - (Actual Quantity Purchased * Standard Unit Cost.)

When the Actual Materials Price is higher than the Standard Materials Price, the variance is said to be unfavorable, since the Actual price paid on materials purchased is greater than the allowed standard. The variance is said to be favorable when the Standard materials Price is higher than the Actual Materials Price, since less money was spent in purchasing the materials than the allowed standard.

- a. Consolidated financial statements
- b. Price Variance
- c. Fund accounting
- d. Liquidating dividend

10. _____ is a 'policy by which management devotes its time to investigating only those situations in which actual results differ significantly from planned results. The idea is that management should spend its valuable time concentrating on the more important items (such as shaping the company's future strategic course.) Attention is given only to material deviations requiring investigation.'

It is not entirely synonymous with the concept of exception management in that it describes a policy where absolute focus is on exception management, in contrast to moderate application of exception management.

- a. Performance measurement
- b. Best practice
- c. Cash cow
- d. Management by exception

11. In business, _____, Overhead cost or _____ expense refers to an ongoing expense of operating a business. The term _____ is usually used to group expenses that are necessary to the continued functioning of the business, but do not directly generate profits.

_____ expenses are all costs on the income statement except for direct labor and direct materials.

a. ABC Television Network
b. Intangible assets
c. AIG
d. Overhead

12. _____ is a common concept in economics, and gives rise to derived concepts such as consumer debt. Generally _____ is defined by opposition to production. But the precise definition can vary because different schools of economists define production quite differently.
a. Starving the beast
b. Mitigating Control
c. Yield
d. Consumption

Chapter 9. Responsibility Accounting

1. In economics, business, retail, and accounting, a _____ is the value of money that has been used up to produce something, and hence is not available for use anymore. In economics, a _____ is an alternative that is given up as a result of a decision. In business, the _____ may be one of acquisition, in which case the amount of money expended to acquire it is counted as _____.
    a. Cost of quality
    b. Prime cost
    c. Cost allocation
    d. Cost

2. _____s are parts of a corporation that directly add to its profit.

    A _____ manager is held accountable for both revenues, and costs (expenses), and therefore, profits. What this means in terms of managerial responsibilities is that the manager has to drive the sales revenue generating activities which leads to cash inflows and at the same time control the cost (cash outflows) causing activities.

    a. Cost driver
    b. Cost management
    c. Profit center
    d. Contribution margin

3. In economics, _____ or _____ goods or real _____ refers to factors of production used to create goods or services that are not themselves significantly consumed (though they may depreciate) in the production process. _____ goods may be acquired with money or financial _____. In finance and accounting, _____ generally refers to financial wealth, especially that used to start or maintain a business.
    a. Screening
    b. Disclosure
    c. Capital
    d. Vyborg Appeal

4. In finance, _____ also known as return on investment, rate of profit or sometimes just return, is the ratio of money gained or lost on an investment relative to the amount of money invested. The amount of money gained or lost may be referred to as interest, profit/loss, gain/loss, or net income/loss. The money invested may be referred to as the asset, capital, principal, or the cost basis of the investment.
    a. Debt to capital ratio
    b. Theoretical ex-rights price
    c. Capital employed
    d. Rate of return

5. _____ is a 'policy by which management devotes its time to investigating only those situations in which actual results differ significantly from planned results. The idea is that management should spend its valuable time concentrating on the more important items (such as shaping the company's future strategic course.) Attention is given only to material deviations requiring investigation.'

It is not entirely synonymous with the concept of exception management in that it describes a policy where absolute focus is on exception management, in contrast to moderate application of exception management.

a. Cash cow
b. Best practice
c. Management by exception
d. Performance measurement

6. _____ is the practical application of management techniques to control and report on the financial health of the organization. This involves the analysis, planning, implementation, and control of programs designed to provide financial data reporting for managerial decision making. This includes the maintenance of bank accounts, developing financial statements, cash flow and financial performance analysis.

a. Activity-based costing
b. Accounting management
c. ABC Television Network
d. Activity-based management

7. _____ is an important property of a control system, and the _____ property plays a crucial role in many control problems, such as stabilization of unstable systems by feedback, or optimal control.

_____ and observability are dual aspects of the same problem.

Roughly, the concept of _____ denotes the ability to move a system around in its entire configuration space using only certain admissible manipulations.

a. Controllable
b. 3M Company
c. BMC Software, Inc.
d. Controllability

8. _____ is the process whereby an organization establishes the parameters within which programs, investments, and acquisitions are reaching the desired results. Performance Reference Model of the Federal Enterprise Architecture, 2005.

Chapter 9. Responsibility Accounting

This process of measuring performance often requires the use of statistical evidence to determine progress toward specific defined organizational objectives.

There are many types of measurements.

a. Performance measurement
b. Management by exception
c. Management by objectives
d. Trustee

9. In business and accounting, _____ are everything of value that is owned by a person or company. It is a claim on the property your income of a borrower. The balance sheet of a firm records the monetary value of the _____ owned by the firm.
   a. Accrual basis accounting
   b. Earnings before interest, taxes, depreciation and amortization
   c. Accounts receivable
   d. Assets

10. In mathematics _____s are numbers or other things that get multiplied. In particular, see:

    - Factorization, the decomposition of an object into a product of other objects
    - Integer factorization, the process of breaking down a composite number into smaller non-trivial divisors
    - A coefficient
    - A divisor of a particular number, or of an element of a monoid
    - A von Neumann algebra with a trivial center

In statistics

- _____ analysis is the study of how _____s or certain variables affect variables.

In technology:

- Human _____s, a profession that focuses on how people interact with products, tools, or procedures
- 'Functionality, Application domain, Conditions, Technology, Objects and Responsibility;', In object-oriented programming

In computer science and information technology:

- Authentication _____, a piece of information used to verify a person's identity for security purposes
- _____, a Unix command for numbers factorization
- _____ (programming language), an experimental Forth-like programming language

In television:

- The O'Reilly _____, an American talk show hosted by Bill O'Reilly on Fox News.
- The Krypton _____, a British game show hosted by Gordon Burns, formally on ITV. Also had an American version.

a. Valuation
b. The Goodyear Tire ' Rubber Company
c. Merck ' Co., Inc.
d. Factor

11. _____ is subcontracting a process, such as product design or manufacturing, to a third-party company. The decision to outsource is often made in the interest of lowering cost or making better use of time and energy costs, redirecting or conserving energy directed at the competencies of a particular business, or to make more efficient use of land, labor, capital, (information) technology and resources. _____ became part of the business lexicon during the 1980s.
   a. Economic Growth and Tax Relief Reconciliation Act of 2001
   b. USA Today
   c. US Airways, Inc.
   d. Outsourcing

12. _____ is one of a series of accounting transactions dealing with the billing of customers who owe money to a person, company or organization for goods and services that have been provided to the customer. In most business entities this is typically done by generating an invoice and mailing or electronically delivering it to the customer, who in turn must pay it within an established timeframe called credit or payment terms.

An example of a common payment term is Net 30, meaning payment is due in the amount of the invoice 30 days from the date of invoice.

a. Accrual
b. Accounts receivable
c. Accrued revenue
d. Adjusting entries

13. _____ is the balance of the amounts of cash being received and paid by a business during a defined period of time, sometimes tied to a specific project. Measurement of _____ can be used

- to evaluate the state or performance of a business or project.
- to determine problems with liquidity. Being profitable does not necessarily mean being liquid. A company can fail because of a shortage of cash, even while profitable.
- to project rate of returns. The time of _____s into and out of projects are used as inputs to financial models such as internal rate of return, and net present value.
- to examine income or growth of a business when it is believed that accrual accounting concepts do not represent economic realities. Alternately, _____ can be used to 'validate' the net income generated by accrual accounting.

_____ as a generic term may be used differently depending on context, and certain _____ definitions may be adapted by analysts and users for their own uses. Common terms include operating _____ and free _____.

a. Commercial paper
b. Controlling interest
c. Flow-through entity
d. Cash flow

14. The _____ is a performance management tool which began as a concept for measuring whether the smaller-scale operational activities of a company are aligned with its larger-scale objectives in terms of vision and strategy.

By focusing not only on financial outcomes but also on the operational, marketing and developmental inputs to these, the _____ helps provide a more comprehensive view of a business, which in turn helps organizations act in their best long-term interests. This tool is also being used to address business response to climate change and greenhouse gas emissions.

a. Management by objectives
b. Trustee
c. Balanced scorecard
d. Best practice

15. In corporate finance, _____ or _____ is an estimate of true economic profit after making corrective adjustments to GAAP accounting, including deducting the opportunity cost of equity capital. _____ can be measured as Net Operating Profit After Taxes(or NOPAT) less the money cost of capital. _____ is similar in nature to that of calculating another financial performance measure - Residual Income , however, there are a few complexities involved with coming up with the elements for calculating _____ over RI such as the myriad adjustments that might be made to NOPAT before it is suitable for the formula below.
   a. Economic value added
   b. International Monetary Fund
   c. Outsourcing
   d. Internal control

16. _____ refers to the additional value of a commodity over the cost of commodities used to produce it from the previous stage of production. An example is the price of gasoline at the pump over the price of the oil in it. In national accounts used in macroeconomics, it refers to the contribution of the factors of production, i.e., land, labor, and capital goods, to raising the value of a product and corresponds to the incomes received by the owners of these factors.
   a. 3M Company
   b. Minimum wage
   c. Supply-side economics
   d. Value added

17. A _____ is an economy based on the division of labor in which the prices of goods and services are determined in a free price system set by supply and demand. This is often contrasted with a planned economy, in which a central government determines the price of goods and services using a fixed price system. Market economies are contrasted with mixed economy where the price system is not entirely free but under some government control that is not extensive enough to constitute a planned economy.
   a. BMC Software, Inc.
   b. BNSF Railway
   c. 3M Company
   d. Market economy

18. _____ is a business management strategy aimed at embedding awareness of quality in all organizational processes. _____ has been widely used in manufacturing, education, call centers, government, and service industries, as well as NASA space and science programs.

Chapter 9. Responsibility Accounting

When used together as a phrase, the three words in this expression have the following meanings:

- Total: Involving the entire organization, supply chain, and/or product life cycle
- Quality: With its usual definitions, with all its complexities
- Management: The system of managing with steps like Plan, Organize, Control, Lead, Staff, provisioning and organizing.

As defined by the International Organization for Standardization (ISO):

'_____ is a management approach for an organization, centered on quality, based on the participation of all its members and aiming at long-term success through customer satisfaction, and benefits to all members of the organization and to society.' ISO 8402:1994

One major aim is to reduce variation from every process so that greater consistency of effort is obtained. (Royse, D., Thyer, B., Padgett D., ' Logan T., 2006)

In Japan, _____ comprises four process steps, namely:

1. Kaizen - Focuses on 'Continuous Process Improvement', to make processes visible, repeatable and measurable.
2. Atarimae Hinshitsu - The idea that 'things will work as they are supposed to' .
3. Kansei - Examining the way the user applies the product leads to improvement in the product itself.
4. Miryokuteki Hinshitsu - The idea that 'things should have an aesthetic quality' (for example, a pen will write in a way that is pleasing to the writer.)

_____ requires that the company maintain this quality standard in all aspects of its business. This requires ensuring that things are done right the first time and that defects and waste are eliminated from operations.

a. BNSF Railway
b. BMC Software, Inc.
c. 3M Company
d. Total quality management

19. _____ in economics and business is the result of an exchange and from that trade we assign a numerical monetary value to a good, service or asset. If Alice trades Bob 4 apples for an orange, the _____ of an orange is 4 apples. Inversely, the _____ of an apple is 1/4 oranges.
    a. Transactional Net Margin Method
    b. Discounts and allowances
    c. Price discrimination
    d. Price

20. _____ is one of the four Ps of the marketing mix. The other three aspects are product, promotion, and place. It is also a key variable in microeconomic price allocation theory.
   a. Target costing
   b. Cost-plus pricing
   c. Price
   d. Pricing

21. _____ refers to the pricing of contributions (assets, tangible and intangible, services, and funds) transferred within an organization. For example, goods from the production division may be sold to the marketing division, or goods from a parent company may be sold to a foreign subsidiary. Since the prices are set within an organization (i.e. controlled), the typical market mechanisms that establish prices for such transactions between third parties may not apply.
   a. Price
   b. Transactional Net Margin Method
   c. Pricing
   d. Transfer pricing

Chapter 10. Planning for Capital Investments

1. In economics, _____ or _____ goods or real _____ refers to factors of production used to create goods or services that are not themselves significantly consumed (though they may depreciate) in the production process. _____ goods may be acquired with money or financial _____. In finance and accounting, _____ generally refers to financial wealth, especially that used to start or maintain a business.
    a. Screening
    b. Capital
    c. Vyborg Appeal
    d. Disclosure

2. In finance, _____ also known as return on investment, rate of profit or sometimes just return, is the ratio of money gained or lost on an investment relative to the amount of money invested. The amount of money gained or lost may be referred to as interest, profit/loss, gain/loss, or net income/loss. The money invested may be referred to as the asset, capital, principal, or the cost basis of the investment.
    a. Rate of return
    b. Debt to capital ratio
    c. Theoretical ex-rights price
    d. Capital employed

3. Simply put, _____ is the value of money figuring in a given amount of interest for a given amount of time. For example 100 dollars of todays money held for a year at 5 percent interest is worth 105 dollars, therefore 100 dollars paid now or 105 dollars paid exactly one year from now is the same amount of payment of money with that given intersest at that given amount of time. This notion dates at least to Martín de Azpilcueta of the School of Salamanca.
    a. Merck ' Co., Inc.
    b. Collusion
    c. Time value of money
    d. Competition law

4. In cost-volume-profit analysis, a form of management accounting, _____ is the marginal profit per unit sale. It is a useful quantity in carrying out various calculations, and can be used as a measure of operating leverage.

The Total _____ is Total Revenue (TR, or Sales) minus Total Variable Cost (TVC):

   Tcontribution margin = TR − TVC

The Unit _____ (C) is Unit Revenue (Price, P) minus Unit Variable Cost (V):

   C = P − V

The _____ Ratio is the percentage of Contribution over Total Revenue, which can be calculated from the unit contribution over unit price or total contribution over Total Revenue:

$$\frac{C}{P} = \frac{P-V}{P} = \frac{\text{Unit Contribution Margin}}{\text{Price}} = \frac{\text{Total Contribution Margin}}{\text{Total Revenue}}$$

For instance, if the price is $10 and the unit variable cost is $2, then the unit _____ is $8, and the _____ ratio is $8/$10 = 80%.

a. Profit center
b. Contribution margin
c. Cost management
d. Factory overhead

5. In economics, business, retail, and accounting, a _____ is the value of money that has been used up to produce something, and hence is not available for use anymore. In economics, a _____ is an alternative that is given up as a result of a decision. In business, the _____ may be one of acquisition, in which case the amount of money expended to acquire it is counted as _____.

a. Prime cost
b. Cost allocation
c. Cost
d. Cost of quality

6. The _____ is an expected return that the provider of capital plans to earn on their investment.

Capital (money) used for funding a business should earn returns for the capital providers who risk their capital. For an investment to be worthwhile, the expected return on capital must be greater than the _____.

a. Capital flight
b. 3M Company
c. BMC Software, Inc.
d. Cost of capital

7. _____ is the value on a given date of a future payment or series of future payments, discounted to reflect the time value of money and other factors such as investment risk. _____ calculations are widely used in business and economics to provide a means to compare cash flows at different times on a meaningful 'like to like' basis.

The most commonly applied model of the time value of money is compound interest.

Chapter 10. Planning for Capital Investments

a. Net present value
b. Future value
c. 3M Company
d. Present value

8. An _____ is a term used in behavioral economics to describe those types of behaviors that impose costs on a person in the long-run that are not taken into account when making decisions in the present. Classical Economics discourages government from creating legislation that targets internalities, because it is assumed that the consumer takes these personal costs into account when paying for the good that causes the _____. For example, cigarettes should be taxed because of the negative consumption externalities that they impose, such as second-hand smoke, not because the smoker harms him or herself by smoking.

a. Internality
b. Operating budget
c. Inventory turnover ratio
d. Authorised capital

9. The term _____ is used in finance theory to refer to any terminating stream of fixed payments over a specified period of time. This usage is most commonly seen in academic discussions of finance, usually in connection with the valuation of the stream of payments, taking into account time value of money concepts such as interest rate and future value.

Examples of these are regular deposits to a savings account, monthly home mortgage payments and monthly insurance payments.

a. Appropriation
b. Annuity
c. Intangible
d. Improvement

10. In mathematics _____s are numbers or other things that get multiplied. In particular, see:

- Factorization, the decomposition of an object into a product of other objects
- Integer factorization, the process of breaking down a composite number into smaller non-trivial divisors
- A coefficient
- A divisor of a particular number, or of an element of a monoid
- A von Neumann algebra with a trivial center

In statistics

- _____ analysis is the study of how _____s or certain variables affect variables.

58   *Chapter 10. Planning for Capital Investments*

In technology:

- Human _____s, a profession that focuses on how people interact with products, tools, or procedures
- 'Functionality, Application domain, Conditions, Technology, Objects and Responsibility;', In object-oriented programming

In computer science and information technology:

- Authentication _____, a piece of information used to verify a person's identity for security purposes
- _____, a Unix command for numbers factorization
- _____ (programming language), an experimental Forth-like programming language

In television:

- The O'Reilly _____, an American talk show hosted by Bill O'Reilly on Fox News.
- The Krypton _____, a British game show hosted by Gordon Burns, formally on ITV. Also had an American version.

a. The Goodyear Tire ' Rubber Company
b. Merck ' Co., Inc.
c. Factor
d. Valuation

11. _____ or net present worth (NPW) is defined as the total present value (PV) of a time series of cash flows. It is a standard method for using the time value of money to appraise long-term projects. Used for capital budgeting, and widely throughout economics, it measures the excess or shortfall of cash flows, in present value terms, once financing charges are met.
    a. Net present value
    b. 3M Company
    c. Future value
    d. Present value

12. _____, in managerial economics is a form of cost accounting. It is a simplified model, useful for elementary instruction and for short-run decisions.

Cost-volume-profit (CVP) analysis expands the use of information provided by breakeven analysis.

Chapter 10. Planning for Capital Investments

a. Cost of quality
b. Fixed costs
c. Cost-volume-profit analysis
d. Cost accounting

13. The _____ is a capital budgeting metric used by firms to decide whether they should make investments. It is also called discounted cash flow rate of return (DCFROR) or rate of return (ROR.) It is an indicator of the efficiency or quality of an investment, as opposed to net present value (NPV), which indicates value or magnitude.

a. AIG
b. AMEX
c. ABC Television Network
d. Internal rate of return

14. _____ is a financial metric which represents operating liquidity available to a business. Along with fixed assets such as plant and equipment, _____ is considered a part of operating capital. It is calculated as current assets minus current liabilities.

a. Working capital
b. Working capital management
c. BMC Software, Inc.
d. 3M Company

15. _____ is the balance of the amounts of cash being received and paid by a business during a defined period of time, sometimes tied to a specific project. Measurement of _____ can be used

- to evaluate the state or performance of a business or project.
- to determine problems with liquidity. Being profitable does not necessarily mean being liquid. A company can fail because of a shortage of cash, even while profitable.
- to project rate of returns. The time of _____s into and out of projects are used as inputs to financial models such as internal rate of return, and net present value.
- to examine income or growth of a business when it is believed that accrual accounting concepts do not represent economic realities. Alternately, _____ can be used to 'validate' the net income generated by accrual accounting.

_____ as a generic term may be used differently depending on context, and certain _____ definitions may be adapted by analysts and users for their own uses. Common terms include operating _____ and free _____.

Chapter 10. Planning for Capital Investments

a. Flow-through entity
b. Commercial paper
c. Controlling interest
d. Cash flow

16. _____ is an important property of a control system, and the _____ property plays a crucial role in many control problems, such as stabilization of unstable systems by feedback, or optimal control.

_____ and observability are dual aspects of the same problem.

Roughly, the concept of _____ denotes the ability to move a system around in its entire configuration space using only certain admissible manipulations.

a. Controllability
b. Controllable
c. BMC Software, Inc.
d. 3M Company

17. _____ are made by investors and investment managers.

Investors commonly perform investment analysis by making use of fundamental analysis, technical analysis and gut feel.

_____ are often supported by decision tools.

a. ABC Television Network
b. Investment decisions
c. AIG
d. Incremental capital-output ratio

Chapter 11. Product Costing in Service and Manufacturing Entities

1. In economics, business, retail, and accounting, a _____ is the value of money that has been used up to produce something, and hence is not available for use anymore. In economics, a _____ is an alternative that is given up as a result of a decision. In business, the _____ may be one of acquisition, in which case the amount of money expended to acquire it is counted as _____.
   a. Cost allocation
   b. Cost
   c. Prime cost
   d. Cost of quality

2. In business, _____, Overhead cost or _____ expense refers to an ongoing expense of operating a business. The term _____ is usually used to group expenses that are necessary to the continued functioning of the business, but do not directly generate profits.

   _____ expenses are all costs on the income statement except for direct labor and direct materials.

   a. Intangible assets
   b. ABC Television Network
   c. AIG
   d. Overhead

3. A _____ is the rate used to apply manufacturing overhead to work-in-process inventory. It is calculated as estimated manufacturing overhead cost divided by estimated amount of cost driver or activity base. Common activity bases used in the calculation include direct labor costs, direct labor hours, or machine hours.
   a. Kaizen
   b. Sensitivity analysis
   c. Procurement
   d. Pre-determined overhead rate

4. _____ are formal records of a business' financial activities.

   In British English, including United Kingdom company law, _____ are often referred to as accounts, although the term _____ is also used, particularly by accountants.

   _____ provide an overview of a business' financial condition in both short and long term.

   a. Notes to the financial statements
   b. 3M Company
   c. Statement of retained earnings
   d. Financial statements

5. Total _____ is a method of Accounting cost which entails the full cost of manufacturing or providing a service. This includes not just the costs of materials and labour, but also of all manufacturing overheads (whether e;fixede; or e;variablee;.) One of the main reasons for absorbing overheads into the cost of units is for inventory valuation purposes.

   a. ABC Television Network
   b. AMEX
   c. AIG
   d. Absorption costing

Chapter 12. Job-Order, Process, and Hybrid Cost Systems

1. In economics, business, retail, and accounting, a _____ is the value of money that has been used up to produce something, and hence is not available for use anymore. In economics, a _____ is an alternative that is given up as a result of a decision. In business, the _____ may be one of acquisition, in which case the amount of money expended to acquire it is counted as _____.
   a. Cost
   b. Cost of quality
   c. Prime cost
   d. Cost allocation

2. A _____ is the transfer of wealth from one party (such as a person or company) to another. A _____ is usually made in exchange for the provision of goods, services or both, or to fulfill a legal obligation.

   The simplest and oldest form of _____ is barter, the exchange of one good or service for another.

   a. 3M Company
   b. Payment
   c. Payee
   d. BMC Software, Inc.

3. _____ is an acronym for First In, First Out, an abstraction in ways of organizing and manipulation of data relative to time and prioritization. This expression describes the principle of a queue processing technique or servicing conflicting demands by ordering process by first-come, first-served (FCFS) behaviour: what comes in first is handled first, what comes in next waits until the first is finished, etc.

   Thus it is analogous to the behaviour of persons queueing (or 'standing in line', in common American parlance), where the persons leave the queue in the order they arrive, or waiting one's turn at a traffic control signal.

   a. Trademark
   b. Risk management
   c. Kanban
   d. FIFO

Chapter 12. Job-Order, Process, and Hybrid Cost Systems

4. _____ is the balance of the amounts of cash being received and paid by a business during a defined period of time, sometimes tied to a specific project. Measurement of _____ can be used

   - to evaluate the state or performance of a business or project.
   - to determine problems with liquidity. Being profitable does not necessarily mean being liquid. A company can fail because of a shortage of cash, even while profitable.
   - to project rate of returns. The time of _____s into and out of projects are used as inputs to financial models such as internal rate of return, and net present value.
   - to examine income or growth of a business when it is believed that accrual accounting concepts do not represent economic realities. Alternately, _____ can be used to 'validate' the net income generated by accrual accounting.

   _____ as a generic term may be used differently depending on context, and certain _____ definitions may be adapted by analysts and users for their own uses. Common terms include operating _____ and free _____.

   a. Commercial paper
   b. Flow-through entity
   c. Controlling interest
   d. Cash flow

Chapter 13. Financial Statement Analysis

1. _____ of a business involves analyzing its financial statements and health, its management and competitive advantages, and its competitors and markets. The term is used to distinguish such analysis from other types of investment analysis, such as quantitative analysis and technical analysis.

_____ is performed on historical and present data, but with the goal of making financial forecasts.

a. Fundamental analysis
b. BNSF Railway
c. 3M Company
d. BMC Software, Inc.

2. _____ refers to an excess amount of information being provided, making processing and absorbing tasks very difficult for the individual because sometimes we cannot see the validity behind the information . As the world moves into a new era of globalization, an increasing number of people are logging onto the internet to conduct their own research and are given the ability to produce as well as consume the data accessed on an increasing number of websites . As of February 2007 there were over 108 million distinct websites and increasing .

a. Information overload
b. AMEX
c. ABC Television Network
d. AIG

3. In mathematics _____s are numbers or other things that get multiplied. In particular, see:

- Factorization, the decomposition of an object into a product of other objects
- Integer factorization, the process of breaking down a composite number into smaller non-trivial divisors
- A coefficient
- A divisor of a particular number, or of an element of a monoid
- A von Neumann algebra with a trivial center

In statistics

- _____ analysis is the study of how _____s or certain variables affect variables.

In technology:

- Human _____s, a profession that focuses on how people interact with products, tools, or procedures
- 'Functionality, Application domain, Conditions, Technology, Objects and Responsibility;', In object-oriented programming

In computer science and information technology:

- Authentication _____, a piece of information used to verify a person's identity for security purposes
- _____, a Unix command for numbers factorization
- _____ (programming language), an experimental Forth-like programming language

In television:

- The O'Reilly _____, an American talk show hosted by Bill O'Reilly on Fox News.
- The Krypton _____, a British game show hosted by Gordon Burns, formally on ITV. Also had an American version.

a. Factor
b. The Goodyear Tire ' Rubber Company
c. Merck ' Co., Inc.
d. Valuation

4. The term _____ is a term applied to practices that are perfunctory, or seek to satisfy the minimum requirements or to conform to a convention or doctrine. It has different meanings in different fields.

In accounting, _____ earnings are those earnings of companies in addition to actual earnings calculated under the Generally Accepted Accounting Principles (GAAP) in their quarterly and yearly financial reports.

a. Bottom line
b. Pro forma
c. Treasury stock
d. Payroll

5. The term '_____' refers to the concept of collecting information and attempting to spot a pattern in the information. In some fields of study, the term '_____' has more formally-defined meanings.

In project management _____ is a mathematical technique that uses historical results to predict future outcome.

a. Trend analysis
b. Regression analysis
c. Multicollinearity
d. 3M Company

6. In financial accounting, a _____ or statement of financial position is a summary of a person's or organization's balances. Assets, liabilities and ownership equity are listed as of a specific date, such as the end of its financial year. A _____ is often described as a snapshot of a company's financial condition.

a. Financial statements
b. Statement of retained earnings
c. 3M Company
d. Balance sheet

7. _____ is a company's financial statement that indicates how the revenue is transformed into the net income The purpose of the _____ is to show managers and investors whether the company made or lost money during the period being reported.

The important thing to remember about an _____ is that it represents a period of time.

a. AMEX
b. AIG
c. ABC Television Network
d. Income statement

8. In economics, _____ or _____ goods or real _____ refers to factors of production used to create goods or services that are not themselves significantly consumed (though they may depreciate) in the production process. _____ goods may be acquired with money or financial _____. In finance and accounting, _____ generally refers to financial wealth, especially that used to start or maintain a business.

a. Vyborg Appeal
b. Screening
c. Disclosure
d. Capital

9. The _____ is a financial ratio that measures whether or not a firm has enough resources to pay its debts over the next 12 months. It compares a firm's current assets to its current liabilities. It is expressed as follows:

$$\text{Current ratio} = \frac{\text{Current Assets}}{\text{Current Liabilities}}$$

Chapter 13. Financial Statement Analysis

For example, if WXY Company's current assets are $50,000,000 and its current liabilities are $40,000,000, then its _____ would be $50,000,000 divided by $40,000,000, which equals 1.25.

a. Net Interest Income
b. Times interest earned
c. Current ratio
d. Return on capital

10. _____ is a business, economics or investment term that refers to an asset's ability to be easily converted through an act of buying or selling without causing a significant movement in the price and with minimum loss of value. Money, or cash on hand, is the most liquid asset. An act of exchange of a less liquid asset with a more liquid asset is called liquidation.

a. Transfer agent
b. Spot rate
c. Financial instruments
d. Market liquidity

11. _____ is a financial metric which represents operating liquidity available to a business. Along with fixed assets such as plant and equipment, _____ is considered a part of operating capital. It is calculated as current assets minus current liabilities.

a. 3M Company
b. Working capital management
c. BMC Software, Inc.
d. Working capital

12. In economics, business, retail, and accounting, a _____ is the value of money that has been used up to produce something, and hence is not available for use anymore. In economics, a _____ is an alternative that is given up as a result of a decision. In business, the _____ may be one of acquisition, in which case the amount of money expended to acquire it is counted as _____.

a. Cost
b. Prime cost
c. Cost allocation
d. Cost of quality

13. In finance, the _____ or quick ratio or liquid ratio measures the ability of a company to use its near cash or quick assets to immediately extinguish or retire its current liabilities. Quick assets include those current assets that presumably can be quickly converted to cash at close to their book values.

Chapter 13. Financial Statement Analysis

$$\text{Quick (Acid Test) Ratio} = \frac{\text{Cash} + \text{Marketable Securities} + \text{Accounts Receivables}}{\text{Current Liabilities}}$$

Generally, the acid test ratio should be 1:1 or better, however this varies widely by industry.

a. Invested capital
b. Inventory turnover
c. Earnings per share
d. Acid-test

14. _____ is one of a series of accounting transactions dealing with the billing of customers who owe money to a person, company or organization for goods and services that have been provided to the customer. In most business entities this is typically done by generating an invoice and mailing or electronically delivering it to the customer, who in turn must pay it within an established timeframe called credit or payment terms.

An example of a common payment term is Net 30, meaning payment is due in the amount of the invoice 30 days from the date of invoice.

a. Accounts receivable
b. Accrual
c. Adjusting entries
d. Accrued revenue

15. _____ is that which is owed; usually referencing assets owed, but the term can also cover moral obligations and other interactions not requiring money. In the case of assets, _____ is a means of using future purchasing power in the present before a summation has been earned. Some companies and corporations use _____ as a part of their overall corporate finance strategy.

a. Loan
b. Debenture
c. Lender
d. Debt

16. The _____ is a financial ratio indicating the relative proportion of equity to all used to finance a company's assets. The two components are often taken from the firm's balance sheet or statement of financial position (so-called book value), but the ratio may also be calculated using market values for both, if the company's equities are publicly traded.

The _____ is especially in Central Europe a very common financial ratio while in the US the debt to _____ is more often used in financial (research) reports.

a. Equity ratio
b. Efficiency ratio
c. Average accounting return
d. Earnings yield

17. The _____ is an equation that equals the cost of goods sold divided by the average inventory. Average inventory equals beginning inventory plus ending inventory divided by 2.

The formula for _____:

$$\text{Inventory Turnover} = \frac{\text{Cost of Goods Sold}}{\text{Average Inventory}}$$

The formula for average inventory:

$$\text{Average Inventory} = \frac{\text{Beginning inventory} + \text{Ending inventory}}{2}$$

A low turnover rate may point to overstocking, obsolescence, or deficiencies in the product line or marketing effort.

a. Upside potential ratio
b. Inventory turnover
c. Earnings per share
d. Enterprise Value/Sales

18. In business and accounting, _____ are everything of value that is owned by a person or company. It is a claim on the property your income of a borrower. The balance sheet of a firm records the monetary value of the _____ owned by the firm.

a. Accounts receivable
b. Earnings before interest, taxes, depreciation and amortization
c. Accrual basis accounting
d. Assets

19. In finance, or business _____ is the ability of an entity to pay its debts with available cash. _____ can also be described as the ability of a corporation to meet its long-term fixed expenses and to accomplish long-term expansion and growth. The better a company's _____, the better it is financially.

a. Solvency
b. Capital asset
c. BMC Software, Inc.
d. 3M Company

20. In economic models, the _____ time frame assumes no fixed factors of production. Firms can enter or leave the marketplace, and the cost (and availability) of land, labor, raw materials, and capital goods can be assumed to vary. In contrast, in the short-run time frame, certain factors are assumed to be fixed, because there is not sufficient time for them to change.
a. Long-run
b. BMC Software, Inc.
c. Short-run
d. 3M Company

21. _____ are liabilities with a future benefit over one year, such as notes payable that mature greater than one year.

In accounting, the _____ are shown on the right wing of the balance-sheet representing the sources of funds, which are generally bounded in form of capital assets.

Examples of _____ are debentures, mortgage loans and other bank loans (note: not all bank loans are long term as not all are paid over a period greater than a year, the example is bridging loan.)

a. Long-term liabilities
b. Cash basis accounting
c. Gross sales
d. Book value

22. _____ is a fee paid on borrowed assets. It is the price paid for the use of borrowed money, or, money earned by deposited funds. Assets that are sometimes lent with _____ include money, shares, consumer goods through hire purchase, major assets such as aircraft, and even entire factories in finance lease arrangements. The _____ is calculated upon the value of the assets in the same manner as upon money.
a. Insolvency
b. ABC Television Network
c. AIG
d. Interest

Chapter 13. Financial Statement Analysis

23. In financial accounting, a _____ is defined as an obligation of an entity arising from past transactions or events, the settlement of which may result in the transfer or use of assets, provision of services or other yielding of economic benefits in the future.
    a. Corporate governance
    b. False Claims Act
    c. Vested
    d. Liability

24. _____ is a financial ratio that measures the efficiency of a company's use of its assets in generating sales revenue or sales income to the company.

$$Asset\ Turnover = \frac{Sales}{Average Total Assets}$$

- 'Sales' is the value of 'Net Sales' or 'Sales' from the company's income statement
- 'Average Total Assets' is the value of 'Total assets' from the company's balance sheet in the beginning and the end of the fiscal period divided by 2.

    a. Enterprise Value/Sales
    b. Average propensity to consume
    c. Information ratio
    d. Asset turnover

25. In business, _____, operating income margin, operating profit margin or return on sales (ROS) is the ratio of operating income (operating profit in the UK) divided by net sales, usually presented in percent.

$$Operating\ margin = \left(\frac{Operating\ income}{Revenue}\right)$$

(Relevant figures in italics)

$$Operating\ margin = \left(\frac{6,318}{24,088}\right) = \underline{26.23\%}$$

It is a measurement of what proportion of a company's revenue is left over, before taxes and other indirect costs (such as rent, bonus, interest, etc.), after paying for variable costs of production as wages, raw materials, etc. A good _____ is needed for a company to be able to pay for its fixed costs, such as interest on debt.

a. Omega ratio
b. Asset turnover
c. Average accounting return
d. Operating margin

26. In business, operating margin, operating income margin, operating profit margin or _____ is the ratio of operating income (operating profit in the UK) divided by net sales, usually presented in percent.

$$\text{Operating margin} = \left(\frac{\text{Operating income}}{\text{Revenue}}\right)$$

(Relevant figures in italics)

$$\text{Operating margin} = \left(\frac{6,318}{24,088}\right) = \underline{\underline{26.23\%}}$$

It is a measurement of what proportion of a company's revenue is left over, before taxes and other indirect costs (such as rent, bonus, interest, etc.), after paying for variable costs of production as wages, raw materials, etc. A good operating margin is needed for a company to be able to pay for its fixed costs, such as interest on debt.

a. Debt service coverage ratio
b. Total revenue share
c. Diluted Earnings Per Share
d. Return on sales

27. A _____ is the pinnacle activity involved in selling products or services in return for money or other compensation. It is an act of completion of a commercial activity.

A _____ is completed by the seller, the owner of the goods.

a. Maturity
b. Tertiary sector of economy
c. Sale
d. High yield stock

Chapter 13. Financial Statement Analysis

28. In finance, _____ also known as return on investment, rate of profit or sometimes just return, is the ratio of money gained or lost on an investment relative to the amount of money invested. The amount of money gained or lost may be referred to as interest, profit/loss, gain/loss, or net income/loss. The money invested may be referred to as the asset, capital, principal, or the cost basis of the investment.
   a. Capital employed
   b. Debt to capital ratio
   c. Theoretical ex-rights price
   d. Rate of return

29. _____ measures the rate of return on the ownership interest (shareholders' equity) of the common stock owners. It measures a firm's efficiency at generating profits from every dollar of shareholders' equity (also known as net assets or assets minus liabilities.) It shows how well a company uses investment dollars to generate earnings growth.
   a. Like for like
   b. Return on Equity
   c. Sortino ratio
   d. Return on capital employed

30. In accounting, _____ or carrying value is the value of an asset according to its balance sheet account balance. For assets, the value is based on the original cost of the asset less any depreciation, amortization or impairment costs made against the asset. Traditionally, a company's _____ is its total assets minus intangible assets and liabilities.
   a. Book value
   b. Depreciation
   c. Generally accepted accounting principles
   d. Matching principle

31. _____ is a specific term used in companies' financial reporting from the company-whole point of view. Because that use excludes the effects of changing ownership interest, an economic measure of _____ is necessary for financial analysis from the shareholders' point of view

_____ is defined by the Financial Accounting Standards Board, or FASB, as 'the change in equity [net assets] of a business enterprise during a period from transactions and other events and circumstances from nonowner sources. It includes all changes in equity during a period except those resulting from investments by owners and distributions to owners.'

_____ is the sum of net income and other items that must bypass the income statement because they have not been realized, including items like an unrealized holding gain or loss from available for sale securities and foreign currency translation gains or losses.

a. BNSF Railway
b. 3M Company
c. BMC Software, Inc.
d. Comprehensive income

32. _____ are the earnings returned on the initial investment amount.

In the US, the Financial Accounting Standards Board (FASB) requires companies' income statements to report _____ for each of the major categories of the income statement: continuing operations, discontinued operations, extraordinary items, and net income.

The _____ formula does not include preferred dividends for categories outside of continued operations and net income.

a. Earnings yield
b. Invested capital
c. Average accounting return
d. Earnings per share

33. A _____ is any one of a variety of different systems, institutions, procedures, social relations and infrastructures whereby persons trade, and goods and services are exchanged, forming part of the economy. It is an arrangement that allows buyers and sellers to exchange things. _____s vary in size, range, geographic scale, location, types and variety of human communities, as well as the types of goods and services traded.
a. Perfect competition
b. Recession
c. Market Failure
d. Market

34. The _____ of a stock is a measure of the price paid for a share relative to the annual net income or profit earned by the firm per share. It is a financial ratio used for valuation: a higher _____ means that investors are paying more for each unit of net income, so the stock is more expensive compared to one with lower _____. The _____ has units of years, which can be interpreted as 'number of years of earnings to pay back purchase price', ignoring the time value of money.
a. Rate of return
b. Sharpe ratio
c. Capital employed
d. P/E ratio

Chapter 13. Financial Statement Analysis

35. _____ in economics and business is the result of an exchange and from that trade we assign a numerical monetary value to a good, service or asset. If Alice trades Bob 4 apples for an orange, the _____ of an orange is 4 apples. Inversely, the _____ of an apple is 1/4 oranges.
    a. Discounts and allowances
    b. Transactional Net Margin Method
    c. Price discrimination
    d. Price

36. _____ are payments made by a corporation to its shareholder members. It is the portion of corporate profits paid out to stockholders. When a corporation earns a profit or surplus, that money can be put to two uses: it can either be re-invested in the business (called retained earnings), or it can be paid to the shareholders as a dividend.
    a. Dividend yield
    b. Dividends
    c. Dividend payout ratio
    d. Dividend stripping

37. The _____ on a company stock is the company's annual dividend payments divided by its market cap, or the dividend per share divided by the price per share. It is often expressed as a percentage.

    Dividend payments on preferred shares are stipulated by the prospectus.

    a. Dividend payout ratio
    b. Dividends
    c. Dividend stripping
    d. Dividend yield

38. In finance, the term _____ describes the amount in cash that returns to the owners of a security. Normally it does not include the price variations, at the difference of the total return. _____ applies to various stated rates of return on stocks (common and preferred, and convertible), fixed income instruments (bonds, notes, bills, strips, zero coupon), and some other investment type insurance products (e.g. annuities.)
    a. Residence trusts
    b. Disclosure
    c. Pension System
    d. Yield

39. In economics, _____ are business expenses that are not dependent on the activities of the business They tend to be time-related, such as salaries or rents being paid per month. This is in contrast to variable costs, which are volume-related (and are paid per quantity.)

In management accounting, _____ are defined as expenses that do not change in proportion to the activity of a business, within the relevant period or scale of production.

a. Cost of quality
b. Marginal cost
c. Cost accounting
d. Fixed costs

40. A _____ is the transfer of wealth from one party (such as a person or company) to another. A _____ is usually made in exchange for the provision of goods, services or both, or to fulfill a legal obligation.

The simplest and oldest form of _____ is barter, the exchange of one good or service for another.

a. BMC Software, Inc.
b. 3M Company
c. Payee
d. Payment

Chapter 14. Statement of Cash Flows

1. In financial accounting, a _____ or Statement of cash flows is a financial statement that shows a company's flow of cash. The money coming into the business is called cash inflow, and money going out from the business is called cash outflow. The statement shows how changes in balance sheet and income accounts affect cash and cash equivalents, and breaks the analysis down to operating, investing, and financing activities.

   a. BMC Software, Inc.
   b. BNSF Railway
   c. 3M Company
   d. Cash flow statement

2. _____ is the balance of the amounts of cash being received and paid by a business during a defined period of time, sometimes tied to a specific project. Measurement of _____ can be used

   - to evaluate the state or performance of a business or project.
   - to determine problems with liquidity. Being profitable does not necessarily mean being liquid. A company can fail because of a shortage of cash, even while profitable.
   - to project rate of returns. The time of _____s into and out of projects are used as inputs to financial models such as internal rate of return, and net present value.
   - to examine income or growth of a business when it is believed that accrual accounting concepts do not represent economic realities. Alternately, _____ can be used to 'validate' the net income generated by accrual accounting.

   _____ as a generic term may be used differently depending on context, and certain _____ definitions may be adapted by analysts and users for their own uses. Common terms include operating _____ and free _____.

   a. Commercial paper
   b. Flow-through entity
   c. Controlling interest
   d. Cash flow

3. _____ of something is, in finance, the adding together of interest or different investments over a period of time such as atoms (1 - the act or process of accruing; 2 - the amount that accrues.) It holds specific meanings in accounting and payroll.

   _____, in accounting, describes the accounting method known as _____ basis, whereby revenues and expenses are recognized when they are accrued, i.e. accumulated (earned or incurred), regardless when the actual cash is received or paid out.

   a. Accounts receivable
   b. Accrual
   c. Assets
   d. Earnings before interest, taxes, depreciation and amortization

Chapter 14. Statement of Cash Flows

4. _____ is a method of accounting whereby economic activities (rather than cash flow) of financial events are considered, because of two complementary principles, which (together) determine the point, at which expenses and revenues are recognized. According to revenue recognition principle, revenues are realized when earned, whether or not they are received in cash.

   a. Accrual basis accounting
   b. Earnings before interest, taxes, depreciation and amortization
   c. Accrual
   d. Accrued revenue

5. _____ is a method of accounting whereby cash flow of financial events is considered. The method recognizes revenues when cash is received and recognizes expenses when cash is paid out. In cash accounting, revenues and expenses are also called cash receipts and cash payments respectively.

   a. Closing entries
   b. Net sales
   c. Cash basis accounting
   d. Treasury stock

6. In accounting, _____ has a very specific meaning. It is an outflow of cash or other valuable assets from a person or company to another person or company. This outflow of cash is generally one side of a trade for products or services that have equal or better current or future value to the buyer than to the seller.

   a. AIG
   b. ABC Television Network
   c. AMEX
   d. Expense

7. The term _____, derived from the distinctive T shape, is frequently used when discussing or analyzing accounting or business transactions. _____s are used to represent general ledger accounts.

   Typically one or more Ts are drawn on a white board or blank piece of paper. A general ledger account name or number is then written above each T. Debit entries are recorded on the left side of the 'T' and credit entries are recorded on the right side of the 'T'.

   a. 3M Company
   b. T account
   c. BNSF Railway
   d. BMC Software, Inc.

Chapter 14. Statement of Cash Flows

8. In economics, business, retail, and accounting, a _____ is the value of money that has been used up to produce something, and hence is not available for use anymore. In economics, a _____ is an alternative that is given up as a result of a decision. In business, the _____ may be one of acquisition, in which case the amount of money expended to acquire it is counted as _____.
   a. Cost
   b. Cost allocation
   c. Prime cost
   d. Cost of quality

9. A _____ is the pinnacle activity involved in selling products or services in return for money or other compensation. It is an act of completion of a commercial activity.

   A _____ is completed by the seller, the owner of the goods.

   a. High yield stock
   b. Maturity
   c. Tertiary sector of economy
   d. Sale

10. A _____ is the transfer of wealth from one party (such as a person or company) to another. A _____ is usually made in exchange for the provision of goods, services or both, or to fulfill a legal obligation.

    The simplest and oldest form of _____ is barter, the exchange of one good or service for another.

    a. BMC Software, Inc.
    b. Payee
    c. Payment
    d. 3M Company

11. In financial accounting, _____ or cost of sales includes the direct costs attributable to the production of the goods sold by a company. This amount includes the materials cost used in creating the goods along with the direct labor costs used to produce the good. It excludes indirect expenses such as distribution costs and sales force costs.
    a. Reorder point
    b. FIFO and LIFO accounting
    c. 3M Company
    d. Cost of goods sold

Chapter 14. Statement of Cash Flows

12. _____ is a term used in accounting, economics and finance to spread the cost of an asset over the span of several years.

In simple words we can say that _____ is the reduction in the value of an asset due to usage, passage of time, wear and tear, technological outdating or obsolescence, depletion, inadequacy, rot, rust, decay or other such factors.

In accounting, _____ is a term used to describe any method of attributing the historical or purchase cost of an asset across its useful life, roughly corresponding to normal wear and tear.

   a. Depreciation
   b. Current asset
   c. General ledger
   d. Net profit

13. _____, in law and economics, is a form of risk management primarily used to hedge against the risk of a contingent loss. _____ is defined as the equitable transfer of the risk of a loss, from one entity to another, in exchange for a premium, and can be thought of as a guaranteed small loss to prevent a large, possibly devastating loss. An insurer is a company selling the _____; an insured is the person or entity buying the _____.
   a. AMEX
   b. Insurance
   c. ABC Television Network
   d. AIG

14. An _____, operating expenditure, operational expense, operational expenditure or OPEX is an on-going cost for running a product, business, or system. Its counterpart, a capital expenditure (CAPEX), is the cost of developing or providing non-consumable parts for the product or system. For example, the purchase of a photocopier is the CAPEX, and the annual paper and toner cost is the OPEX.
   a. AMEX
   b. ABC Television Network
   c. AIG
   d. Operating expense

15. In business, _____, Overhead cost or _____ expense refers to an ongoing expense of operating a business. The term _____ is usually used to group expenses that are necessary to the continued functioning of the business, but do not directly generate profits.

_____ expenses are all costs on the income statement except for direct labor and direct materials.

Chapter 14. Statement of Cash Flows

   a. AIG
   b. Overhead
   c. Intangible assets
   d. ABC Television Network

16. _____ is a fee paid on borrowed assets. It is the price paid for the use of borrowed money, or, money earned by deposited funds .Assets that are sometimes lent with _____ include money, shares, consumer goods through hire purchase, major assets such as aircraft, and even entire factories in finance lease arrangements. The _____ is calculated upon the value of the assets in the same manner as upon money.
   a. Insolvency
   b. AIG
   c. ABC Television Network
   d. Interest

17. _____ are securities that can be easily converted into cash. Such securities will generally have highly liquid markets allowing the security to be sold at a reasonable price very quickly.This is a usual feature in real estate .
   a. BMC Software, Inc.
   b. 3M Company
   c. Tracking stock
   d. Marketable

18. An _____ is the buying of one company by another. An _____ may be friendly or hostile. In the former case, the companies cooperate in negotiations; in the latter case, the takeover target is unwilling to be bought or the target's board has no prior knowledge of the offer. _____ usually refers to a purchase of a smaller firm by a larger one. Sometimes, however, a smaller firm will acquire management control of a larger or longer established company and keep its name for the combined entity. This is known as a reverse takeover.
   a. ABC Television Network
   b. Acquisition
   c. AMEX
   d. AIG

19. A _____ is a fungible, negotiable instrument representing financial value. they are broadly categorized into debt securities (such as banknotes, bonds and debentures), and equity securities; e.g., common stocks. The company or other entity issuing the _____ is called the issuer.

Chapter 14. Statement of Cash Flows

a. BMC Software, Inc.
b. Security
c. Tracking stock
d. 3M Company

20. In finance, a _____ is a debt security, in which the authorized issuer owes the holders a debt and, depending on the terms of the _____, is obliged to pay interest (the coupon) and/or to repay the principal at a later date, termed maturity. It is a formal contract to repay borrowed money with interest at fixed intervals.

Thus a _____ is like a loan: the issuer is the borrower, the _____ holder is the lender, and the coupon is the interest.

a. Bond
b. Zero-coupon bond
c. Revenue bonds
d. Coupon rate

21. _____ are payments made by a corporation to its shareholder members. It is the portion of corporate profits paid out to stockholders. When a corporation earns a profit or surplus, that money can be put to two uses: it can either be re-invested in the business (called retained earnings), or it can be paid to the shareholders as a dividend.

a. Dividends
b. Dividend yield
c. Dividend payout ratio
d. Dividend stripping

Chapter 1

1. d	2. d	3. d	4. c	5. b	6. a	7. a	8. c	9. d	10. c
11. d	12. d	13. c	14. d	15. c	16. d	17. b	18. b	19. a	20. d
21. c	22. d	23. b	24. c	25. d	26. b	27. b	28. d	29. d	30. c
31. b	32. a	33. a	34. d	35. b	36. b	37. d	38. c	39. b	40. d
41. b	42. d	43. d	44. c						

Chapter 2

| 1. d | 2. a | 3. c | 4. d | 5. b | 6. d | 7. d | 8. b | 9. d | 10. d |
| 11. d | | | | | | | | | |

Chapter 3

| 1. d | 2. c | 3. c | 4. d | 5. b | 6. d | 7. a | 8. c | 9. d | 10. a |
| 11. a | 12. d | 13. d | 14. d | 15. d | 16. d | 17. b | 18. d | | |

Chapter 4

| 1. c | 2. b | 3. b | 4. d | 5. d | 6. c | 7. d | 8. b | 9. a | 10. c |
| 11. d | 12. c | 13. d | 14. c | | | | | | |

Chapter 5

1. d	2. d	3. a	4. d	5. a	6. d	7. a	8. c	9. b

Chapter 6

| 1. d | 2. d | 3. b | 4. d | 5. d | 6. d | 7. b | 8. b | 9. a | 10. c |
| 11. d | 12. b | 13. b | 14. c | | | | | | |

Chapter 7

| 1. c | 2. d | 3. c | 4. d | 5. a | 6. b | 7. a | 8. c | 9. d | 10. d |
| 11. d | 12. d | 13. d | 14. d | 15. d | 16. b | 17. a | | | |

Chapter 8

| 1. c | 2. b | 3. c | 4. a | 5. c | 6. b | 7. d | 8. c | 9. b | 10. d |
| 11. d | 12. d | | | | | | | | |

Chapter 9

1. d	2. c	3. c	4. d	5. c	6. b	7. d	8. a	9. d	10. d
11. d	12. b	13. d	14. c	15. a	16. d	17. d	18. d	19. d	20. d
21. d									

Chapter 10

| 1. b | 2. a | 3. c | 4. b | 5. c | 6. d | 7. d | 8. a | 9. b | 10. c |
| 11. a | 12. c | 13. d | 14. a | 15. d | 16. a | 17. b | | | |

Chapter 11

1. b	2. d	3. d	4. d	5. d

ANSWER KEY

Chapter 12
    1. a   2. b   3. d   4. d

Chapter 13
    1. a   2. a   3. a   4. b   5. a   6. d   7. d   8. d   9. c   10. d
    11. d   12. a   13. d   14. a   15. d   16. a   17. b   18. d   19. a   20. a
    21. a   22. d   23. d   24. d   25. d   26. d   27. c   28. d   29. b   30. a
    31. d   32. d   33. d   34. d   35. d   36. b   37. d   38. d   39. d   40. d

Chapter 14
    1. d   2. d   3. b   4. a   5. c   6. d   7. b   8. a   9. d   10. c
    11. d   12. a   13. b   14. d   15. b   16. d   17. d   18. b   19. b   20. a
    21. a

www.ingramcontent.com/pod-product-compliance
Lightning Source LLC
Chambersburg PA
CBHW081848230426
43669CB00018B/2865